THE STATE AND RELIGION

IN A NUTSHELL

By

THOMAS C. BERG

Professor of Law
Samford University,
Cumberland School of Law

**WEST
GROUP**

ST. PAUL, MINN.
1998

COPYRIGHT © 1998 By WEST GROUP
                    610 Opperman Drive
                    P.O. Box 64526
                    St. Paul, MN 55164–0526
                    1–800–328–9352

Library of Congress Cataloging-in-Publication Data
Berg, Thomas C., 1960–
    The state and religion in a nutshell / by Thomas C. Berg.
        p.   cm.
    Includes index.
    ISBN 0–314–22663–X (pbk.)
    1. Church and state—United States.   I. Title.
KF4865.Z9B47   1998
344.73'096—dc21   97–51739
                                                                            CIP

ISBN 0–314–22663–X

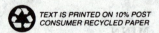

PREFACE

My thinking about the basic concepts of religious freedom discussed in this book has been much influenced by Professor Michael McConnell, who taught me the Religion Clauses of the First Amendment at the University of Chicago Law School ten years ago. He has also been a valued friend and advisor, as well as a colleague in writing and litigating about church-state disputes. He is not, of course, responsible for what I have written here. My colleagues at Cumberland Law School, William Ross, David Smolin and Stephen Ware, read the manuscript and gave helpful comments. So did my wife, Maureen Kane Berg, who is a careful thinker, a superb lawyer, a devoted mother, and a loving and supportive life partner.

THOMAS C. BERG

Birmingham, Alabama
January, 1998

*

OUTLINE

OUTLINE

OUTLINE

OUTLINE

TABLE OF CASES

References are to Pages

TABLE OF CASES

TABLE OF CASES

TABLE OF CASES

*

THE STATE AND AND RELIGION
IN A NUTSHELL

*

CHAPTER ONE

AN INTRODUCTORY OVERVIEW

Early in 1988, reporters asked presidential candidate George Bush about a formative ordeal in his youth: the days he had spent marooned at sea in World War II after the fighter plane he piloted was shot down over the Pacific. Bush answered that he had kept his strength by thinking about "things that really matter, like God and faith"—and, he quickly added, "the separation of church and state." Reporters chuckled at the thought of Bush taking comfort in fond memories of Supreme Court opinions about church and state.

However absurd his statement was, Bush had instinctively reflected the attitude of a great many Americans concerning the relationship of government to religion. We have been, and despite many predictions continue to be, a people with a strong religious strain. A large majority of Americans want their government and its officials, at least to some extent, to reflect and be guided by religious faith and principles (in a recent Gallup poll, more than 65 percent said they would be reluctant to vote for an atheist for president). At the same time, most Americans want the state not to become too involved in religious affairs—an attitude that is expressed sometimes in the idea of separation between church and state, and sometimes simply in the idea of religious liberty. Some observers think that there is a tension between the notion that government should be influenced by religious values and the notion that government should stay out of religious matters itself. Other observers think that the two ideas are perfectly compatible. And people disagree sharply on where to draw the line between permissible and impermissible government action concerning religion, as well as on the reasons for drawing the line.

The question of how the state should treat religious beliefs and practices is an age-old one. For much of human history, societies thought it crucial that all citizens be uniform in matters of religion— by coercion if necessary—both to preserve social unity and to protect the true religion from attack. The last 400 years in Western Europe and the United States have seen a slow movement toward greater freedom for a wider range of faiths, not just the Christian majority. That process has stemmed from a variety of forces, including the fact of increased religious diversity, the influence of the Enlightenment with its skepticism about many Christian dogmas, and the beliefs of many Christians themselves that a coerced faith is neither real nor effective. There are still deep disagreements about how the state should treat religion, but they seldom lead to coercion or violence in the United States today.

Nevertheless, the disagreements are deep and important. Government will always face questions about how far religious freedom extends when religious practice conflicts with social duties or the rights of others. An even deeper issue, however, is that broad freedom for all religious beliefs and groups may be purchased at the price of divorcing religion entirely from public life. Some critics say that this has happened in recent years, that the American tradition of "separation of church and state" has been turned into a separation of government from religious norms and values. This, they say, is very dangerous because religion is an indispensable source of moral guidance and discipline, particularly in a nation with such a high level of religious identification in its population as the United States (polls still show that more than 90 percent of Americans believe in a God).

In recent decades, many of these questions have become matters of constitutional law addressed by the U.S. Supreme Court and other courts. The primary legal vehicle has been the First Amendment to the Constitution, which as currently interpreted prohibits all levels of government from making any law "respecting an establishment of religion or prohibiting the free exercise thereof."

The Supreme Court's decisions in this area have provided some of the most controversial instances of the power of judicial review (that is, the power to disregard a laws because it conflicts with the Constitution). The Court has invalidated some long-standing relationships between government and religion, such as state-sponsored school prayer, and as a result some observers claim that the justices have disregarded the original purposes of the First Amendment and have suppressed the role of religion in public affairs. But the Court has also upheld various government actions affecting religion, especially in recent years, often in ways that appear to conflict with its previous decisions or statements. Critics on all sides are united in agreeing that the case law is internally inconsistent, some say incoherent.

This chapter introduces the major themes of this book. It summarizes the constitutional provisions on religion, provides a suggested framework for analyzing issues concerning the state and religion, and briefly describes the the general legal standards that the Supreme Court has followed under the two Religion Clauses, free exercise and non-establishment.

A. THE FIRST AMENDMENT AND OTHER LEGAL PROVISIONS

1. The Religious Test Clause

The original Constitution, before the subsequent amendments, contained one provision concerning religion. Article VI, section 3 provides that "no religious test shall ever be required as a qualification to any office or public trust under the United States." This clause prohibited for the new federal government the practice, still followed then in most of the states, of requiring officeholders to swear a belief in God or in particular religious doctrines.

Under current case law, the Religious Test Clause is superfluous, because the Supreme Court has held that religious tests for government office fall within the prohibitions of the First Amendment. *Torcaso v. Watkins* (S.Ct.1961) (striking down a state requirement that officials declare belief in God). The Court relied on the First Amendment because the case involved a state law. As discussed below, the Amendment has come to cover state and local laws by virtue of its incorporation in the Fourteenth Amendment. By contrast, it is hard to read the Religious Test Clause, because of its language and history, as covering anything other than offices in the federal government.

2. The First Amendment

The religion provision of the First Amendment is part of the Bill of Rights, the ten amendments that were added in 1791 to provide extra assurance that the new federal government would not interfere with the prerogatives of state governments or with the liberties of citizens. The religion provision states: "Congress shall make no law respecting an establishment of religion, or prohibiting the free exercise thereof." Courts and commentators often refer to these as two separate religion clauses— nonestablishment and free exercise—and analyze cases as falling under one clause or the other. But other commentators argue that the two clauses must be read in light of each other rather than in isolation, to harmonize rather than conflict; after all, the clauses were enacted simultaneously as a single statement about church and state.

Religious activity often takes the form of speech or other expression: a sermon, an evangelistic rally in a public park, a book or tract of doctrine. Such cases also implicate the other portion of the First Amendment, which prohibits any law "abridging the freedom of speech," of the press, or of assembly. Many modern decisions protecting religious freedom have done so through interpretation of the Free Speech Clause.

3. Incorporation of the First Amendment

Like the rest of the Bill of Rights, the First Amendment as enacted applied only to the federal government. *Barron v. Mayor and City Council of Baltimore* (S.Ct.1833). How then does the modern Court review local government actions such as school board policies on classroom prayer? The answer is that since the mid–20th century, the Court has held that the religion and speech clauses are "incorporated" into the Fourteenth Amendment as part of its provision prohibiting states from denying any person "due process of law." See, e.g., *Gitlow v. New York* (S.Ct.1925) (free speech); *Cantwell v. Connecticut* (S.Ct.1940) (free exercise); *Everson v. Board of Education* (S.Ct.1947) (non-establishment). Of course, most of the restrictions of the Bill of Rights have been applied to state and local governments in this fashion.

There is little or no prospect that the Court will retreat from the incorporation doctrine, in religion or in any other area. Freedom of religion is now among the fundamental rights that most Americans assume government at all levels should respect. But the doctrine has been controversial. Some scholars still claim that the Fourteenth Amendment, which was passed shortly after the Civil War in 1868, was intended only to guarantee black Americans certain civil rights such as the right to marry, make contracts, and own property. Others read the Due Process Clause more broadly, but still say that it protects only certain "fundamental" rights, which would include some basic features of religious freedom but not necessarily all those entailed in the provisions of the First Amendment.

A few critics attack the incorporation of the Religion Clauses in particular. Some point to the proposed Blaine Amendment of 1875, which failed to pass Congress but which would have explicitly amended the Constitution to apply the nonestablishment and free exercise rules to state governments. Why would Congress even consider such a proposal, the critics ask, if it had meant just a few years earlier to apply the First Amendment to states? Defenders of incorporation respond that the Blaine Amendment may have been thought necessary, even if the Fourteenth Amendment had been intended to incorporate the Religion Clauses, because the Supreme Court had eviscerated the Amendment in the interim in the *Slaughter–House Cases* (S.Ct.1873). Incorporation defenders also assert that there may have been other factors that explain why the Blaine Amendment was proposed, and why it failed as well. In any event, some incorporation defenders say, the meaning of the Fourteenth Amendment is not bounded by the drafters' specific goals.

Other critics argue that the original purpose of the Religion Clauses, especially nonestablishment, was simply to prevent the new federal government from interfering with the religious policies of state governments, several of whom still had established churches in 1791. (Note that the Establishment Clause prohibits any law "respecting an establishment of religion," which may include attempts to interfere with state establishments.) Such a "state's rights" policy cannot logically be applied to restrict state governments.

Defenders of incorporation respond that the Religion Clauses were meant to protect individual rights as well, and that for this purpose the extension of the provision to restrict infringements by state government makes sense. *Abington School District v. Schempp* (S.Ct.1963) (Brennan, J., concurring). In addition, religious freedom in some form was probably on the minds of the Reconstruction Congress that drafted the Fourteenth Amendment: a chief criticism of the South's slavery regime had been that it restricted the religious activity of slaves and of missionaries who tried to preach to them.

4. Other Provisions

The federal Constitution is not the only relevant law, for states have their own constitutional provisions concerning religion. Some, as we will see, restrict government action more stringently than the Religion Clauses do. Moreover, provisions concerning religion can be found throughout the vast range of statutes and regulatory codes, both federal and state. Laws or regulations may exempt churches from taxes or regulations, or forbid churches from receiving government financial assistance. Such provisions also reflect a policy on how the state should treat religion. Their interaction with constitutional rules is one of the recurring subjects of this book.

B. THE INTERPRETATION OF THE RELIGION CLAUSES: A SUGGESTED FRAMEWORK FOR UNDERSTANDING

Although this book contains historical and other discussions, its main purpose is to explain and analyze modern judicial decisions concerning the government and religion. Because the Supreme Court's case law has often appeared shifting and inconsistent, a student or practitioner in this area needs a framework with which to categorize and analyze various rulings, and this book aims to provide such a framework. Needless to say, it will not explain everything, but it can help in understanding. First, though, a few words about general issues in constitutional interpretation and how they apply to religion cases.

1. Constitutional Interpretation in General

When judges engage in judicial review of legislation, they appeal to the constitutional text as supreme law enacted by the people (see the Supremacy Clause of Article VI, section 2). Without such authority, federal judicial review conflicts with two foundations of the American constitutional system. One is popular rule or democracy, for federal judicial review involves unelected judges overturning laws passed by elected officials. The other is federalism: our system presumes that state governments have power to act except where the Constitution or other federal law withdraws it from them.

The problem, of course, lies in determining what the Constitution means as applied to particular disputed issues. With broadly-worded provisions such as the Religion Clauses, the literal text will not give decisive guidance in some of the most important cases. To what other source(s) should judges look in interpreting the text? This is a complicated subject on which constitutional theorists have staked out many positions. For present purposes, however, we can identify two key approaches to determining the meaning of a constitutional provision such as the Religion Clauses. The goal here is not resolve which approach is best, but only to note briefly the major arguments made for and against each one.

One approach concentrates on determining the historical meaning of the provision as it was understood by the generation in which it was enacted, or perhaps more specifically by the people who actually drafted or ratified it. Defenders of this **original understanding** approach argue that it is only the original meaning that has the authority to override later majority actions, because it alone was enacted by a super-majority through approved legal procedures (such as the procedures for constitutional amendments in Article V).

Against this view, defenders of what might be called a **"moral understanding"** of the Constitution insist that the document reflects certain general principles of political morality—in the case of the First Amendment, freedom of religion, conscience, and expression. These principles, they assert, must be translated in the best way into current circumstances, whatever the understanding of the drafters or enacters might have been. Only in this way can the Constitution adapt to the great changes in the nation that occur over decades and centuries.

We can illustrate some of the issues concerning these two views by examining some problems that each of them raises under the Religion Clauses. Critics of the original understanding view claim that if it confines constitutional doctrine to what the framers specifically thought about particular disputes, it prevents the values of the document from being adapted to materially different circumstances. On the other hand, they say, if the original understanding of a provision is to be understood as some abstract principle that lay behind the framers' specific judgments, then originalism loses much of the certainty that it promised: we will have to choose among general principles, at various levels of abstraction, and perhaps disregard the founders' opinions on specific issues.

For example, the First Amendment's framers seemingly had little problem with explicitly Christian prayers at public events, probably because there were few non-Christians to object, at least in positions of authority. But the framers did more generally want to keep government from taking sides on contentious religious matters, which at the time of founding meant matters in dispute between Protestant bodies. In modern times, when so many more Americans are non-Christian, preserving this more general principle may require overriding the founders' more specific acceptance or tolerance of Christian prayers.

On the other hand, critics of the moral understanding approach claim that without some focus on the understanding of those who enacted a provision, there is no way to give the provision any objective content. In any important case, the moral arguments for and against either position are numerous, uncertain, and dependent on one's perspective. Inevitably, it is asserted, judges who try to follow the "best" moral understanding will simply end up enforcing their own preferences. As such these unelected judges will undermine both democracy and federalism: the right of people to make decisions through their elected representatives and to make decisions at their own local level.

For example, disputes about the proper relationship of the state and religion—or about a particular issue like official prayers in public schools—run very deep and stem from different views about the truth and importance of religion or particular religious beliefs. What a judge thinks is the best understanding of religious freedom is likely to be highly personal to that judge. In particular, some critics argue that the Court's modern Religion Clause decisions reflect the bias of a secularized elite (including the justices and their law clerks) for whom religion usually is not an important or guiding force in life.

These two views are not stark alternatives. The original understanding usually reflects some moral principle, and originalists typically agree that there must be some flexibility in applying such a principle to modern circumstances. On the other side, defenders of the moral approach to the Constitution usually recognize that history will shed considerable light on the underlying principle reflected in a provision, as well as how best to implement it today. Moreover, many ways have been suggested to combine the two views or compromise between them. For example, some have suggested that judges look to fundamental American traditions in order to permit constitutional doctrine to develop without making it turn on the subjective views of unaccountable judges. Here we can only note these issues as they relate to the Religion Clauses, and not resolve them.

2. Potential Religion Clause Values

To try to understand the Religion Clauses and the decisions interpreting them, one must think about what underlying principles or values the clauses and decisions should serve. (For an originalist, the question is what values the clauses were meant to serve historically; for other constitutional theorists, the question is what values the clause should be interpreted now to serve). At bottom, of course, the purpose of the religion provision is "to promote and assure the fullest possible scope of religious liberty and tolerance for all [persons] and to nurture the conditions which secure the best hope of attainment of that end." *Schempp*, *supra* (Goldberg, J., concurring). But religious freedom is not a self-defining concept, and the confusion in the case law reflects the justices' disagreement about what religious freedom means.

The underlying principles or values should explain both clauses, nonestablishment and free exercise. As noted above, the two are part of one provision, almost certainly meant to be harmonious rather than clashing, and so to interpret one in isolation from the other can create difficulties. What posture do the two clauses, taken together, require government to adopt toward religion?

Three principles or values have competed for primacy in answering that question: separation, equality, and religious liberty or choice. See, e.g., *Walz v. Tax Commission* (S.Ct.1970) (Harlan, J., concurring) (discussing values of "voluntarism" or liberty, "neutrality" or equality, and "noninvolvement" or separation). Each of these principles contains some ambiguity itself; each can be construed in a rather limited sense that is widely accepted, but also in a stronger sense that is more controversial. The Supreme Court has not adhered to any one of these values consistently, and that is one major reason that its decisions have been inconsistent. Identifying the values cannot resolve every issue, but it can at least help one to understand and organize the Court's patchwork of decisions.

a. Separation of Church and State

One possible value at which the two Religion Clauses are aimed is the **separation of church and state**. At the minimum, this means not only that church and state are two different institutions (as opposed to a theocracy like Iran), but also that neither state nor church should have any official role in directing the internal governance of the other. We have rejected, for example, the practices of nations with established churches such as Great Britain, where the government has an official (though now almost entirely symbolic) part in choosing church leaders, and bishops have official seats in the upper house of Parliament. The "institutional separation" of church and state, though quite a new step at the time of the founding, is generally accepted in modern America. But a much more ambitious separation of government from religion has been reflected in some modern court decisions, and it has been very controversial.

Beginning in 1947 with *Everson v. Board of Education, supra*, the Court often stated that the First Amendment erects a "wall of separation," quoting a phrase that Thomas Jefferson, then President, used in a letter to some Connecticut Baptists in 1802. The "wall" metaphor has implied not just that religion and government should stay out of each other's internal affairs, but that there should be little or no contact between the two at all. In practice, the Court has used the concept to forbid religious practices in government, such as state-sponsored school prayers, as well as tax-supported government funding of private religious schools.

In these controversial decisions, separation has meant keeping religious activity and influences out of government, primarily to protect citizens of minority faiths or of no faith. The history of governmental assaults on unfamiliar or unpopular beliefs has led many to conclude that religious minorities can only be protected by a strictly secular government. In some cases this position has been based on the contention that religion is an especially sensitive or divisive subject, or that it is particularly hard to resolve religious disagreements empirically or rationally. As a result, it is argued, there should be limits on the extent to which religious issues and differences are brought into the political system. And, it is argued, religion need not enter heavily into political or governmental matters, for government's role is properly confined to secular goals and policies.

However, another tradition of separationism, stemming from the Baptist leader Roger Williams (see Chapter 2), emphasizes the protection of religion more than the protection of society or of the political system. This tradition claims that even "friendly" contacts between church and state end up weakening the purity and strength of religion. The Court has occasionally appealed to this tradition to strike down certain attempts by government to regulate religious bodies—even striking down government's attempts to aid religious institutions such as schools on the ground that with the aid would come government regulation that would compromise the institutions' independence (see Chapter 5).

It has been always impossible to maintain a complete lack of contact between religion and government, since both are concerned with matters of public morality. While there has almost always been a basic institutional separation of church and state throughout American history, government has also in many ways endorsed the dominant faith of Christianity. But sealing off contacts between religion and government has become even more difficult in the last 50 years as the scope of government's activities has grown dramatically, in education and in commercial and welfare regulation. Many critics claim that as government's scope has expanded, requiring government to be strictly secular would mean pushing religion to the margins of public life.

b. Equal Treatment

A second possible Religion Clause value is that of **equal treatment or nondiscrimination**. In this view, the major evil at which the clauses are directed is government's favoring one position over others on matters of religion. When government favors one such position, it treats non-adherents of that position as second-class citizens, and it may allow the favored group to develop a dangerous amount of power. Religious factions of this sort were among those that James Madison, in the Federalist Papers (No. 10), feared would cause social and political strife.

The uncontroversial version of equal treatment is that one religious denomination should not be preferred over others; the Court has called this the "clearest command" of the Religion Clauses. *Larson v. Valente* (S.Ct.1982). The more controversial proposition, however, is that that religion should not be favored over nonreligion.

The Court often refers to the principle of equality as one of "neutrality" among religions or between religion and nonreligion. As Justice Harlan has explained, the neutrality approach basically involves "an equal protection mode of analysis." *Walz v. Tax Commission*, *supra* (concurring opinion). Under the equality ideal, different treatment of citizens or groups on the basis of religion, when the two citizens or groups are otherwise comparable, can be justified only under the narrowest circumstances. A citizen's religious beliefs, or her lack thereof, should be irrelevant to governmental decisions, much as one's race or gender should be irrelevant to the government.

In recent years the Supreme Court has placed more and more emphasis on the equal treatment value, and less on church-state separation. The shift has appeared most notably in two areas: (1) the Court's holding that religious conduct may constitutionally be subjected to the same laws as the rest of society, no matter how great the burden on religion (see Chapter 3); and (2) the Court's approval of more and more forms of government aid to religious organizations on the same terms as to other organizations (see Chapter 5). These holdings stand in tension with earlier decisions that had protected religious practice from some general laws, and that on the other hand had forbidden many forms of government aid to religion, in order to maintain a strong church-state separation. The change in decisions shows that in a time of active government, there may be a conflict between the values of separation (keeping religion distinctively apart from government) and equality (treating religion the same as other beliefs or activities).

c. *Noncoercion and Religious Choice*

A final cluster of values that could underlie the religion provisions is that of **religious liberty, noncoercion, and religious choice**. Under this outlook, the primary goal of the Religion Clauses is to preserve religious liberty, and that goal should be pursued directly—even if on some occasions it involves creating some contact between church and state (in violation of separation), or treating religion differently from other ideas or activities (in violation of equal treatment). Advocates of the religious liberty value often argue that nondiscrimination and church-state separation are simply means for securing the fundamental value of religious liberty, and that these instrumental values should not be followed if they conflict with liberty in a particular case.

Many advocates of this position argue that religious activity is a positive human and social good that the government may or should take specific steps to respect or facilitate. Some emphasize that religious practice should be protected from infringement because it involves duties to a power higher than the state, duties to God or a divine moral authority. But, the religious liberty defenders generally say, government should not try to pressure non-believers into accepting religious truth, because such efforts cannot produce real faith and because they tend instead to call religion into disrepute.

At the least, then, the ideal of religious liberty means that government should not directly coerce anyone to practice or not practice a religion. See *Lee v. Weisman* (S.Ct.1992) (describing this as the "minimum" content of the Establishment Clause). But this limited "noncoercion" principle is consistent with the proposition that government may endorse or give aid to religion in ways that do not coerce dissenting views. Thus, for centuries the notion of religious freedom in the West meant giving toleration to various faiths but still maintaining an established or preferred church. And even in the United States, the ideal of religious freedom for many decades included government support and approval of the Christian or "Judeo–Christian" faiths, together with noncoercion and toleration of dissenters. In fact, some people argue that unless the government is permitted to acknowledge the majority religion in these ways, the liberty of members of the majority faith is restricted.

However, a broader notion of religious liberty would emphasize that government should not try to affect religious choice even in ways that do not involve direct coercion. (James Madison, for example, emphasized that "toleration" was an inadequate substitute for full religious liberty.) The Court has often adopted this position, holding for example that a state-sponsored school prayer is an imposition upon dissenting students even if they are not officially required to participate in it. Professor Douglas Laycock has described this as a "substantive" rather than "formal" neutrality toward religion: neutral not in the sense of treating religion just like anything else (equal treatment), but in the sense of trying to avoid affecting religious choice (a goal that may sometimes call for treating religion distinctively).

* * *

In the America of 1791—a time of limited government and a relatively homogeneous, mostly Protestant population—the three values of separation, equality, and liberty could often work together. For the government to maintain a "hands off" posture toward religious activity and institutions would promote not only church-state separation and religious liberty, but also reasonable equality of treatment between religion and other activities, because the government's regulatory role was limited in general. Moreover, with a general Protestant ethos underlying society, government could remain separate from any particular church and yet the citizenry's general religious values could still contribute to public life.

This is not to say, of course, that these three values were always respected throughout early American history. Unpopular faiths were singled out for disabilities or active suppression: Quakers and Baptists in the colonial period, Catholics at various times, Mormons in the mid-to late 1800s. The only point here is that it was theoretically easier in earlier times for the government to pursue all three values at once.

Now, however, because of changed circumstances, the three values listed above often clash, at least if each is pursued to its logical conclusion. One reason is that active, welfare-state government now regulates and affects nearly all areas of life, from operating schools to regulating commercial activity to subsidizing various social policies. As a result, for example, maintaining church-state separation or religious liberty in the face of regulation may require treating religion quite differently from other activities. And as government grows in size and scope, it becomes more and more difficult to avoid any contacts with religion (the strict separation value), unless religion is treated as an entirely private matter—and to confine religion to the private sphere can involve both discrimination against religion and restrictions on full religious liberty.

Another complicating factor is the increased pluralism in American religion, with many people now self-consciously claiming to be adherents of nontheistic religions or of no religion. To give perfectly equal treatment to all positions on religion that are held by Americans, government may have no choice but to say nothing about religion at all. Yet some critics claim that such a result treats religion less favorably than other ideas that government is permitted to espouse, that it interferes with religious citizens' liberty to try to influence their government, and that it is inconsistent with American history.

The conflict between different principles emerged dramatically in very first modern Establishment Clause case, *Everson*, *supra*. A public school board, using tax-supported funds, reimbursed parents for the cost of sending their children to school on county buses and included parents of parochial school children in the program. The Supreme Court began its discussion with the "wall of separation" metaphor, insisting that the barrier between church and state must be kept "high and impregnable." As a consequence, the Court said, "[n]o tax in any amount, large or small, may be levied to support any religious activities or institutions, whatever they may be called." The majority seemed poised to use the strict separation principle to strike down any aid to religiously affiliated education.

Yet the majority then turned around and upheld the bus reimbursements. Because the state also paid for the cost of transporting public school students, the reimbursement to parochial school families was simply part of a "general program" that helped to carry students to and from school "regardless of their religion." The Religion Clauses did not authorize the state to exclude students, "because of their faith, ... from receiving the benefits of public welfare legislation." The Establishment Clause should not be read to "hamper [ ] citizens in the free exercise of their own religion." School transportation was like other "general government services" such as police or fire protection; to deny these to churches would make the state their "adversary" rather than a "neutral" as it should be. "State power is no more to be used so as to handicap religions than it is to favor them."

The dissenting justices were incredulous that the majority could permit the aid after its discourse on strict separation. But *Everson* revealed that the modern practice of providing funds for the general welfare could create conflicts between the values of separation, on one hand, and equality and religious choice on the other. (Providing benefits to all citizens arguably minimizes the government's effect on religious choice—although the Court has also sometimes argued that using tax-supported funds amounts to coercing some taxpayers to support religions with which they disagree. See Chapter 5 for discussion.)

What the majority failed to do in *Everson* was to make a clear selection of which value was primary. It opted for equality in its result but pointed toward strict church-state separation in its language. And the Court has continued to waver between the different values. For a number of years it gave prime place to separation, but recently it has emphasized equality and choice more frequently. We will trace the course of these developments through several specific areas of church-state law.

C. AN OVERVIEW OF FREE EXER-CISE AND ESTABLISHMENT CLAUSE STANDARDS

Before we begin to discuss particular areas of dispute, it is worth undertaking a brief introduction to the standards that the Court has applied under the First Amendment's two religion provisions, free exercise and non-establishment. We will try to connect these general standards to the three underlying values introduced in the previous section. Later chapters will examine how these standards apply in particular contexts.

1. Free Exercise Clause Standards

Although standards of analysis under the Free Exercise Clause will be examined in detail in Chapter 3, they can briefly be summarized here. The Court has been very concerned to protect religious belief, worship, and expression. Pure religious belief, not manifested in conduct toward others, is absolutely shielded from punishment or regulation by government. Religious speech also receives strong protection, particularly against efforts to limit it simply because the viewpoint expressed is religious. Free exercise protection for religious speech is bolstered by the Free Speech Clause, which generally prohibits government from restricting speech based on its content or viewpoint unless there is a compelling reason to do so and the restriction is narrowly drawn. In recent years, the Court has often applied this analysis to hold that religious speech need not be, and in many cases must not be, singled out for exclusion from government institutions (public schools, squares, and so forth).

In the above categories, the values of separation, equal treatment, and religious liberty generally work in harmony. Protecting religious belief or expression on the same terms as other beliefs also leaves such activities free and keeps government from becoming involved with them.

Conduct motivated by religious faith, however, has presented more difficulties than belief or speech. Conduct can cause physical harm to others in ways that mere belief or expression cannot—consider, for example, a religious cult practicing human sacrifice—and so it must be restricted in some cases. Yet religious faith typically involves more than a just holding and expressing beliefs; it also imposes duties on believers to act, or refrain from acting, in certain ways. When these duties collide with government regulation, what is the result?

The Court has been clear that although government may restrict conduct, it may not single out conduct for restriction simply because it is religious. Such discriminatory action against religious exercise violates the principle of equality as well as religious liberty. But when religious conduct is not singled out for prohibition, but merely collides with a general standard of conduct imposed on all citizens, the Court's approach has been less consistent.

For many years beginning with *Sherbert v. Verner* (S.Ct.1963), the Court held, at least in theory, that when religious duties conflict with a general law, the government is constitutionally required to accommodate the believer's conscience—to exempt him from the law—unless restricting the believer's freedom is necessary to serve a compelling governmental interest. Such accommodations are arguably necessary, at least sometimes, if religious liberty is to be preserved in the face of pervasive governmental regulation; and exemptions from regulation also might be said to serve the goal of keeping church and state separate.

However, religious accommodations achieve these goals at the cost of treating religion differently from other reasons for acting—perhaps even from other conscientious reasons for acting. Many observers have criticized that departure from the principle of equal treatment between religion and other activities. Some have claimed that it conflicts with the Establishment Clause by favoring religion; others say that such favoritism at least means that exemptions should not be constitutionally required.

In *Employment Division v. Smith* (S.Ct.1990), the Court departed from its previous course and ruled that an accommodation in the face of a neutral and generally applicable law is almost never required by the Free Exercise Clause, no matter how minimal the government's interest. This change of standard has significant implications: legislatures seldom single out religious conduct for prohibition, but religious believers and groups often face conflicts between their religious duties and the duties imposed by society's general laws.

The *Smith* standard does not say that legislatures are forbidden to accommodate religious conscience, only that they are not constitutionally required to make such exemptions. The new rule thus focuses on equality more than religious liberty, although it allows legislatures to give distinctive protection to religious liberty as a matter of their own discretion. (*Smith* and its implications will be considered in detail in Chapter 3.)

2. Establishment Clause Standards

Standards of analysis under the Establishment Clause have been more complicated for the Court to develop. Indeed, for several years now there has been no single standard that a majority of the justices has accepted as drawing the proper line between permissible government support for religion and impermissible establishment.

a. The Lemon Test

For many years, the Court followed a three-part Establishment Clause test set forth in *Lemon v. Kurtzman* (S.Ct.1971). In order to satisfy the Establishment Clause under *Lemon*, a law had to have (1) a secular purpose and (2) a primary effect that neither advanced nor inhibited religion, and it could not (3) create excessive entanglement between church and state. Under this test, the Court struck down government-sponsored prayers, Bible readings, and other religious exercises and symbols in the public schools. It also prohibited many, though not all, forms of tax-supported aid to religiously affiliated schools.

As will be discussed in detail in later chapters, these decisions treated the value of church-state separation as the primary goal of the Establishment Clause. *Lemon* required that government remain "neutral" toward religion, neither advancing nor inhibiting it, for the two main reasons generally given for strong church-state separation. First, when government becomes involved in religion or takes a position on religious matters, it excludes those citizens (usually a minority) "who do not adhere to the favored beliefs." *Weisman, supra* (Blackmun, J., concurring) (defending the *Lemon* test). Second, as the tradition stemming from Roger Williams emphasizes, "religion flourishes in greater purity, with than without the aid of government." *Id.*

However, several justices as well as many commentators became dissatisfied with the *Lemon* test, for two chief reasons. First, the test became too easily manipulated, so that standards such as "a primary effect that neither advances nor inhibits religion" came to lose whatever clear meaning they originally had. For example, the Court ruled that tax-supported funding programs that gave aid directly to religiously affiliated schools had the primary effect of advancing religion, but that there was no such impermissible effect when the funds were provided to families who could choose to use them at religious schools. (See Chapter 5 for details.) There may be good reasons to distinguish the two situations, but the "primary effect" standard seemed to serve more as a label than as a tool or guide for analysis.

Second, critics of *Lemon* argued that the test was hostile to religious exercise and to historic traditions of religious involvement in public life. By requiring, as its most important prong, that a law neither advance nor inhibit religion, the test sought to maintain government "neutrality" toward religion. But some critics claim that government cannot be neutral toward religion: since religious ideas offer an important and widely-held perspective on morality and justice, to require the government to refrain from advancing them treats religious ideas less favorably than others. It also runs counter to many specific historical traditions of governmental endorsement of religious faith: indeed, some of our founding documents of religious freedom themselves rest on explicitly religious premises. Critics of *Lemon* on this score particularly attacked the Court's decisions that forbade public schools to conduct religious exercises or display religious symbols even when dissenting students were excused from participating (see Chapter 4).

In addition, some critics say that *Lemon* has been applied in a way that is not really neutral toward religion. For example, in decisions about aid to religiously affiliated schools, *Lemon*'s "primary effect" prong was read to forbid any aid that might be used for a religious purpose, and therefore to bar many kinds of aid to religious schools (see Chapter 5). Critics argue, however, that since government already aids the competitors to religious schools—subsidizing public schools, and at least sometimes secular private schools—the provision of similar aid to religious schools would not "advance" religion in the sense of favoring it over other choices. Indeed, critics argue, to deny educational aid simply because the school in question is religious "inhibits" religion and interferes with the free exercise of families that want a religiously informed education.

The Court has not officially rejected the *Lemon* test, but it has more and more looked to alternatives. Several major candidates have been suggested in recent decisions.

b. No Preference Among Religions

Some scholars, together with Justice Rehnquist, have suggested that the Establishment Clause forbids no more than preferential support of one religious denomination, and that it allows support for religion in general over other ideas or activities. See, e.g., *Wallace v. Jaffree* (S.Ct.1985) (Rehnquist, J., dissenting). Essentially, this position would limit the scope of the Establishment Clause to the most non-controversial version of equality: that equality between religious denominations or sects be re-

spected. Proponents defend this "no sect preference" test primarily on historical grounds, by pointing to a number of actions by the early federal
government giving support or endorsement to general, nondenominational Christianity. *Id.*

Opponents have responded on historical grounds
as well, arguing, among other things, that the
founding generation repeatedly rejected financial
aid for churches even when it was made available to
all denominations. See the discussion in Chapter 2;
see also *Weisman* (Souter, J., concurring). The no-
sect-preference test has never commanded a majority in a modern Supreme Court opinion.

c. No Endorsement

Under another major alternative, the "no-endorsement" test, government would be forbidden
from sending a message that religious beliefs are
endorsed or disapproved by government. See *Lynch
v. Donnelly* (S.Ct.1984) (O'Connor, J., concurring)
(first proposing the test). This approach has commanded a majority in at least one recent decision
(*County of Allegheny v. American Civil Liberties
Union* (S.Ct.1989)), but it has not become fixed as
the governing standard.

The endorsement test does not appear to differ
greatly from *Lemon*, since it likewise emphasizes
that government promotion of religious beliefs excludes those citizens who do not believe them. *Id.*
But, as Justice O'Connor argued in *Lynch*, the non-
endorsement rule may be clearer than the *Lemon*
test because it states more precisely in just what

way government is forbidden to advance or inhibit religion. On the other hand, some critics say that the endorsement test is too subjective because it focuses on government "messages," which different people may read in different ways.

d. Non–Coercion

A more substantial change from *Lemon* would be the "non-coercion" test, under which government could promote religion as long as it did not force anyone to profess religion or participate in a religious ceremony. See, e.g., *Allegheny, supra* (Kennedy, J., concurring) (proposing a similar test). This test would make non-coercion, as opposed to separation, the sole value underlying the Religion Clauses. If applied strictly, it would overrule the decisions prohibiting noncompulsory prayers or other exercises in public schools. The non-coercion test is favored by those who believe that the separation-based approach of *Lemon* conflicts with historical traditions and undercuts religion's role in public life.

Those who oppose the non-coercion test do so, not surprisingly, on the grounds that support church-state separation. They also argue that to limit the Establishment Clause to cases of coercion would make it redundant, since the Free Exercise Clause already prohibits government from forcing anyone to practice or not practice a religion. Several justices have been willing to limit the Establishment Clause to cases of coercion, but no majority has ever done so.

e. Neutrality as Equal Treatment

Finally, recent decisions have increasing focused on a test of "neutrality," but understood in a somewhat different sense from *Lemon*: not that government may give no aid to religion, but that government may not treat religious ideas or citizens differently from non-religious counterparts. This approach—which Professor Laycock calls "formal" neutrality—is increasingly visible in recent decisions upholding various forms of government aid provided to religious organizations as long as such aid is provided equally to other comparable organizations (see Chapter 5 for discussion). It is also visible in recent decisions concerning accommodation of religious duties in the face of general laws; the Court has refused to require such accommodations under the Free Exercise Clause (*Employment Division v. Smith, supra*) and has sometimes even forbade them as a form of favoritism under the Establishment Clause (see Chapter 3). This neutrality approach, therefore, appears to coincide with the underlying value of equal treatment of religion and nonreligion.

In short, church-state separation seems to be giving way as the primary Religion Clause value in the Court's decisions, but its ultimate replacement is not clear. Equal treatment has been a prominent principle in recent decisions—but as our more detailed treatment in subsequent chapters chapters will show, the matter is more complicated than that.

CHAPTER TWO

A BRIEF HISTORY OF AMERICAN CHURCH–STATE RELATIONS

Overview

The European settlers of what became the United States included many people who wanted to practice religion free from persecution and free from what they regarded as corrupt Old World churches. Ever since, religion has consistently played an important role in American history. Conversely, that history is important to an understanding of constitutional principles concerning the government and religion. Justice Rutledge once stated that "[n]o provision of the Constitution is more closely tied to or given content by its generating history than the religious clause of the First Amendment." *Everson v. Board of Education* (S.Ct.1947) (Rutledge, J., dissenting). Some critics say that the Court's religion decisions have failed to pay attention to history or give an accurate reading of it; but in any event, it is important to have some understanding of the history of government actions toward religion in the United States.

This chapter reviews that history very generally, but part C gives a more detailed description of the events and debates surrounding the enactment of the First Amendment. Readers who wish to concentrate on the meaning of the enactment history for modern constitutional issues will probably find that section of the chapter the most helpful.

A. THE EUROPEAN BACKGROUND: ESTABLISHMENTS, RESTRICTIONS ON RELIGIOUS DISSENT, AND WARS OF RELIGION

Even as the North American colonists tried to start afresh in the New World, they also brought with them habits from Europe. The history of Europe must be understood in terms of "Christendom." The early Christians were an insular minority, sometimes persecuted by Rome; the New Testament teachings of Jesus and Paul direct or at least assume that Christians will not exercise the power of the state. But the Christian church grew phenomenally, was adopted by the emperor Constantine in 313, and within a few decades after that became the sole official religion of the empire. As more and more of the peoples of Western Europe adopted Christianity (even after Rome fell), the religion also became intertwined with the state because it was the predominant faith of the people and the culture.

The features of an officially established church were set in medieval times and continued even after the Reformation, when there came to be different established churches in different nations.

Among the common features of an established church are: (1) prohibitions or restrictions on freedom of worship for dissenters; (2) other disabilities on dissenters, such as making them ineligible to hold government office; (3) compelled contributions to the support of the established church; and (4) some government jurisdiction over the internal affairs of the church, such as the appointment of leaders or the content of rituals or doctrine.

Such policies have been common for much of Western history, reflecting the principle that government must support the true faith and place restrictions on those who dissent from it. The underlying premises were that unity among the people requires unity in their beliefs about religion, and that those who preach or practice other beliefs cause a spiritual threat by leading people away from the true faith and therefore must be suppressed by force through government. Saint Augustine and many other influential Christian thinkers defended the use of state force against heretics on these and similar grounds.

As the reasons just given show, restrictions on religious dissent can rest on two different motivations: one secular, to preserve social unity or the control of a dominant social group; and one spiritual, to advance the "true" faith and protect it from being undermined.

These interlocking relations between the government and the established church do not necessarily mean that the two make up one institution. An established church is different from both a theocracy, in which religious leaders actually control the government, or a totalitarian state in which religious affairs are simply a department of the government. From the 1100s into the 1300s, Catholic popes and secular emperors waged an important power struggle that resulted in the maintenance of certain separate jurisdictions for church and state: ecclesiastical courts ruled on matters such as family law and inheritances, while secular courts ruled on most other matters. This struggle confirmed that in the Western tradition, even established churches would be separate institutions from the government. Nevertheless, the two institutions have also been intertwined in a variety of ways.

The Protestant Reformation made little immediate change in these conditions. Although Martin Luther and John Calvin criticized the medieval established Church, they both adhered to the notion that government should support the true faith and restrict or even prohibit others. Calvin's Geneva burned Michael Servetus for denying the Trinity. Luther urged that German Jews' property be confiscated and the Jews be expelled from Germany after they refused to convert.

What the Reformation did instead was to create, for the first time, a significant religious division in Western Europe. Wars broke out between Protestants and Catholics. In Germany, these conflicts were temporarily settled in 1555 by the Peace of Augsburg, under which the religion of each principality was determined by the religion of the ruling prince (*cujus regio, ejus religio*, or "whose the rule, his the religion"). This patchwork of Protestant and Catholic states typifies one possible solution to the problem of religious disputes: let each smaller territory determine its religion, and dissenters in one territory can move to a more hospitable one. An analogous solution is reflected in American principle of federalism, under which each state pursues the governmental policies that it prefers. (In matters of religion, the American states once had power to pursue their own policies, but the federalistic solution is not employed now because under current law, all states must obey the principles of the Religion Clauses.)

The Reformation and its conflicts did, however, eventually lead to further steps in the direction of religious freedom. The Protestant and Catholic states of Germany began to extend a limited form of toleration to members of minority faiths, pursuant to the settlement of a new round of religious wars in the 1600s. Moreover, some theological developments in the Reformation fueled the development of religious freedom. Luther's emphasis on the distinction between earthly and spiritual kingdoms offered a theological basis for limiting the role of government over religious conscience. And the Anabaptists, the radical Protestants who preached adult baptism and withdrawal from the world into a closely-knit Christian community, offered a theological vision in which the church could only remain faithful by rejecting association with the coercive and corrupt institution of government. Many of these themes would be picked up by Protestant dissenters fighting for religious liberty in the American colonies in the 1700s.

The Reformation-era conflicts that most affected the American colonists were those in England. The English national church, which broke officially from Rome in 1532–33 when the Pope refused to approve Henry VIII's divorce from his first wife, was an example of yet another variety of establishment: one in which the secular ruler dominated the church. This outlook is called "Erastianism" (based on a probably mistaken attribution to a 16th-century Swiss reformer named Erastus). The king became supreme head of the English church; monasteries and many other church properties were seized for the royal treasury; and the church gave up a number of its legal powers and parliamentary privileges. Royal control was solidfied under Queen Elizabeth I, who secured a temporary peace after Catholics and Protestants had imprisoned and killed each other throughout the 1550s. There was considerable theological latitude within the Church of England, and elements of both Protestantism and Roman Catholicism; but those outside the boundaries, especially Catholics loyal to Rome, were treated severely. Parliamentary legislation dictated the contents of the prayer book, the practices of clergy, and other church matters.

But the theological compromises made by the Church of England did not satisfy the English Puritans, Calvinists in their beliefs, who objected to the Church's secularized character and to its remaining

Catholic elements. The mid–1600s saw the English Civil War, a new round of conflicts between the Puritan-dominated parliament and the Stuart kings who tried to nudge the Church of England in a more Catholic direction; the conflicts were religious as well as political.

B. DIFFERING COLONIAL PATTERNS: ESTABLISHMENTS VERSUS RELIGIOUS FREEDOM

As the thirteen English colonies developed, they came to display three different models of governmental policy toward religion. The most common model was that of an established church with, at first, little or no tolerance of religious dissent. The groups of Puritans who settled in Massachusetts did so in order to practice what they believed to be true Christianity, but for the most part they did not believe in extending religious freedom to other views. Their Congregationalist Church had virtually all the features of an establishment listed above. The authorities banished heretics such as Anne Hutchinson, the Quakers, and the Baptists, and hanged four Quakers who tried to return after being expelled in the 1650s.

European settlement in the southern colonies was led not by Puritan groups but by commercial enterprises, and these merchants simply brought with them the established Church of England. Partly because that Church was latitudinous and partly because supervision was so far away in London, the

Anglican establishment in the South was less vigorous and rigid than New England Puritanism. But it still operated as an establishment and denied religious freedom to dissenters by, for example, withholding licenses for them to preach. As late as 1774, Baptist preachers in Virginia who conducted non-Anglican services were thrown in jail, an action that so enraged the teenage James Madison that he referred to "[t]hat diabolical Hell-conceived principle of persecution."

A second model, found mostly in the middle colonies of New York and New Jersey, was one of practical religious tolerance based on the fact of great religious diversity. New Jersey had no officially established church. In New York, the Anglican Church was established in a few counties, and perhaps technically throughout the state; but with a few exceptions, dissenting Protestants were granted license to preach and worship, and even Quakers and Jews were left unhindered.

Finally, a model of relatively full religious freedom appeared in two unusual colonies, Rhode Island and Pennsylvania. The first was founded in the 1630s by Roger Williams, a devout man who had crossed swords with the Massachusetts establishment and had been banished. Pennsylvania was founded as a haven for Quakers from persecution in England. Rhode Island, whose charter proposed a "lively experiment ... with a fully liberty in religious conscience," granted such liberty to all citizens as long as they did not disturb the "civil peace." Pennsylvania's provision was similar.

Two features of these colonial models of religious freedom should be noted. First, although they were exceptional in not directly restricting worship or requiring religious taxes, even they imposed disabilities that would be shocking today: Rhode Island banned Catholics from public office and Jews from even living in the colony, and Pennsylvania barred non-Christians from office and limited its religious freedom protections to those who believed in "one almighty God."

Second, in both colonies the theory behind granting religious freedom was a religious one. In numerous writings, most notably *The Bloody Tenent of Persecution* (1644), Roger Williams argued that true Christianity was a voluntary matter (compelled faith "stinketh in the nostrils of God," he said) and that state involvement in religion intruded on and corrupted the domain of the church (his image was of the "wilderness" creeping into the "garden"). Williams understood the state's responsibility as enforcing the second half of the Ten Commandments (civil duties against murder, theft, adultery, and so forth), but not the first half (religious duties of acknowledging God, attending worship, and so forth). Up until to the Enlightenment period of the late 1700s (and even to a significant extent after that), the main theory of religious freedom in America was itself grounded in orthodox Christian beliefs.

At first there were relatively few men such as Williams who dissented on Christian grounds from the established churches in their colonies (Congregationalism in New England, Anglicanism in the South). But that began to change in the mid–1700s, when a series of revivals called the Great Awakening swept through the frontier parts of New England, the Middle Colonies, and Virginia. The revivals contributed to the development of greater religious liberty by creating many new members of Baptist and Presbyterian sects who fought against the disabilities placed on them by colonial establishments.

The Great Awakening also provides an early example of the effect of religion on American politics (a subject discussed in Chapter 6). The popular revivals helped start a populist political wave that opposed British rule and thus helped bring on the American Revolution. The revivals also helped give rise to a movement to abolish slavery.

C. THE FOUNDING GENERATION: IN-CREASED FREE EXERCISE, THE END OF RELIGIOUS TAXES, AND THE ADOPTION OF THE FIRST AMENDMENT

Over time, colonies began to relax some of their restrictions on religious freedom and some of the features of their establishments. Such changes occurred throughout the 1700s, but they accelerated during and after the revolution, when the colonies became states.

The first major change was the gradual relaxation of restrictions on worship and activity by the non-established sects. By the 1770s and 1780s, the newly-independent states were writing constitutions that almost uniformly included provisions protecting religious worship and practice unless it interfered with "the peace and safety of the state." Although two states limited these protections to Christians and five others limited them to believers in God, the other states had no such qualifications, suggesting that all faiths would enjoy freedom.

One form of disability on religious dissenters, however, remained common throughout the founding period: religious tests for public office. Although these were banned for the new federal government in the 1789 Constitution, at that very time eleven states banned non-Christians from public office, and four banned Catholics as well. (Virginia had eliminated its test for office by means of Thomas Jefferson's religious freedom statute of 1786.) These restrictions continued into the 20th century in many states, although they usually were relaxed to forbid only non-theists, thus permitting Jews to hold office. (The Supreme Court finally held the remaining tests unconstitutional in *Torcaso v. Watkins* (S.Ct. 1961).)

The second major change, which occurred mostly in the late 1700s, was that states gradually eliminated tax assessments for the support of churches and ministers. This often proceeded in a number of stages, sometimes over several decades. At the outset, some dissenting sects, most commonly Baptists and Quakers, were exempted from paying taxes in several colonies. An alternative intermediate step was to make the assessment nonpreferential or "general": citizens still had to pay the tax, but they could designate it for the denomination of their choice rather than the formerly preferred established church.

Massachusetts, for example, adopted a general assessment in 1780 in an effort to liberalize its policy of support without eliminating it. But although the system was nonpreferential in theory, it provoked constant complaints from Baptists and other dissenters, who had to go through bureaucratic steps to obtain a certificate allowing them to direct their taxes to their own churches. (They also objected in principle to being compelled to support even their own churches.) Still, this system, and similar ones in Connecticut and New Hampshire, were not abolished until decades after the First Amendment was enacted (1833 in Massachusetts, 1818 in Connecticut, and 1817 in New Hampshire).

The most important debate, however, was in Virginia, where a general assessment was proposed in 1785, again as a compromise. Under the proposal, each taxpayer could designate which denomination would receive his tax; Quakers and Mennonites were exempt because they did not have official clergy; and a citizen could even designate no church, in which case the tax would go to a fund for schools. However, Baptists and Presbyterians opposed the bill, and James Madison rallied opposition with his famous "Memorial and Remonstrance Against Religious Assessments." The legislature rejected the assessment, and instead it enacted Thomas Jefferson's religious freedom statute, which gave full religious freedom and eliminated all religious taxes.

Madison's Memorial and Remonstrance is perhaps the best known document in American church-state relations after the First Amendment itself. The petition eloquently weaves together a variety of arguments against state support for religion, and so can act as a survey of the arguments that were important in this cause.

Many of Madison's contentions reflected the religious or theological arguments for religious freedom, advanced by Roger Williams and by the Baptists dissenters in Madison's day. He asserted that duties to the Creator and "Governor of the Universe" were prior, "both in order of time and degree of obligation, to the claims of Civil Society"; that such duties could be directed only by "conviction, not by force"; that the use of religion by the state was "an unhallowed perversion of the means of salvation"; and that establishments had undermined "the purity and efficacy of religion." These arguments paralleled the evangelical Protestant position that religious duties were prior to those of the state, and that true Christianity must be voluntary and free from any corrupting state involvement. Madison may have been influenced by his contact with evangelical Presbyterians while attending Princeton College, especially his contact with the college's president Reverend John Witherspoon, who pressed these arguments for religious liberty and was also a signer of the Declaration of Independence.

Other references in Madison's masterpiece were influenced by the 18th-century Enlightenment outlook that was so strong among the founders. His argument that religion "can be directed only by reason and conviction" recalls the view of Thomas Jefferson and others that the true elements in religion are those that are rational. Madison argued that establishments have tended either "to erect a spiritual tyranny on the ruins of civil authority" or else "uphold[ ] a political tyranny." Government meddling in religion had spilled "torrents of blood" in Europe. All of these arguably reflect the Enlightenment view that disputes over the details of religious doctrine are particularly likely to produce violence, and are unnecessary to the resolution of any legitimate goal of government.

Finally, some of Madison's arguments were simply prudential, based on the fact of religious diversity in Virginia. He warned that the assessment would destroy "moderation and harmony" between sects, that attempts to force religious uniformity had always failed and produced violence, and that productive citizens seeking a peaceful place to live would be inclined to avoid or leave the state if the bill passed. At least one factor in the increasing scope of religious liberty was that the states were becoming more religiously pluralistic, so that no particular establishment would be acceptable to enough citizens.

Each of these kinds of argument—religious, Enlightenment, and pragmatic—played some role in the development of religious freedom in the states (although which one was most important is a matter of debate). Each also played some role in the adoption of the First Amendment from 1789 to 1791.

One of the chief criticisms of the proposed federal Constitution was the absence of a guarantee that the new, strengthened federal government would not infringe in certain matters that had previously been left to the states or to individual freedom. Religion was among the matters most often cited. (The only provision in the original Constitution concerning religion was the one that forbade the federal government from requiring any religious oath for those holding public office.) Defenders of the Constitution argued that a Bill of Rights was unnecessary because the federal government was given no power over matters such as religion in the first place. But the opponents, although they did not succeed in stopping ratification, did succeed in convincing many people of the need for a Bill of Rights.

Among the groups committed to a religious freedom guarantee were the Baptists of Massachusetts and Virginia. In central Virginia, Baptists and Presbyterians gave most of their votes for Congress to James Madison, who supported the new Constitution but who also had pledged to the new sects to work for amendments on religion and other subjects.

Once elected to Congress, Madison initiated the debate by proposing a set of amendments, including two on religion. One provided that "[t]he civil rights of none shall be abridged on account of religious belief or worship, nor shall any national religion be established, nor shall the full and equal rights of conscience be in any manner, or on any pretext, infringed." The second stated that "no State shall violate the equal rights of conscience."

Before discussing Madison's first proposal, which became the basis for the Religion Clauses, we should call attention to the second—which apparently would have guaranteed freedom of conscience against state governments, thus anticipating by 150 years the judicial application of religious freedom guarantees to the states. This provision, remarkably, passed the House; but it was rejected by the Senate, and the First Amendment as enacted clearly bound only the new federal government.

Madison's first proposal was debated briefly and revised in the House, after which it read "Congress shall make no law establishing religion, or to prevent the free exercise thereof, or to infringe the rights of conscience." The Senate then debated the provision and took several votes. On three occasions, it rejected proposals that would have amended the provision to prohibit from Congress from establishing "one religious sect or society in preference to others," or "any particular denomination of religion in preference to another." It also voted to strike out the clause protecting the "rights of conscience" from infringement. Eventually, after a conference meeting, the House and Senate agreed to the ultimate wording: "Congress shall make no law respecting an establishment of religion, or prohibiting the free exercise thereof."

Because the record of enactment debates is sparse, some have questioned how much guidance it can provide to the intended meaning of the Religion Clauses. However, commentators have raised and discussed a few issues relevant to modern cases. For example, it is sometimes argued today that the First Amendment definition of "religion" must be broad enough to protect all conscientious beliefs, not just those that are traditionally religious (see Chapter 7). Some analysts respond, however, that the enacting Congress specifically rejected the protection for "rights of conscience" and retained only the narrower category of "religion." On the other hand, it may be that the framers saw no real difference between the two terms; religion was virtually the only conscientious belief system with which the framers were familiar.

The enactment history may also be relevant to another modern issue: whether, as some argue, the Establishment Clause prohibits only government preference for one religious denomination over another, and permits government to support religion in general over non-religion (see Chapter 1). Proponents of a broader non-establishment theory point out the Senate specifically rejected three proposals that would have prohibited only preferences between sects. But proponents of the narrower principle of "no sect preferences" argue, again, that the language of proposals was not crucial and that other actions by the first Congress show it meant to permit equal support for all religions.

There were numerous such actions by early Congresses and Presidents. The first Congress appointed chaplains to pray at the opening of its daily sessions, paid for chaplains in the military, and appropriated tax money to pay Christian missionaries to educate and proselytize Indian tribes. Several early presidents (including Washington, Adams, and Madison) issued proclamations encouraging the citizenry to give thanks to God; only Jefferson refused to do so (although Madison in later years opined that his earlier actions had been unconstitutional).

As already noted, some justices and modern commentators believe these actions showed that the First Amendment was understood to prohibit only preferential support for one sect and not support for religion in general. See, e.g., *Wallace v. Jaffree* (S.Ct.1985) (Rehnquist, J., dissenting). But proponents of a broader Establishment Clause prohibition argue that these were politically motivated actions that were not subjected to principled examination for their constitutionality. In any event, they say, even if support for general Christian or Judeo–Christian ideas may have been sufficiently non-discriminatory in the 1700s, it cannot be so today when many citizens profess other religions besides Christianity or Judaism, or profess no religion at all. See, e.g., *Lee v. Weisman* (S.Ct.1992) (Souter, J., concurring).

Other commentators believe the pattern of these actions show that the Religion Clauses were meant to forbid only coercive means of supporting religion. This principle can explain the practice of legislative prayers, presidential proclamations, and other forms of religious expression. But at least some of the early measures involved spending money raised from taxes, which can be seen as coercive. (In the words of Jefferson's Virginia religious freedom statute, religious taxes "compel [the dissenter] to furnish contributions of money for the propagation of opinions which he disbelieves and abhors.")

Moving beyond specific actions, do the Religion Clauses reflect some underlying general theory about how the state should treat religion? And if they reflect such a theory, what consequences would it have for interpreting them today? Some analysts have argued that the "religious" or "evangelical" position was the most important: that Americans adopted religious freedom mostly based on Christian principles. Some proponents of this view adopt solely a "non-coercion" view of the clauses, on the basis that religious belief should not be compelled but that it is also valuable and government may support it in ways short of coercion. On the other hand, other proponents of the religious view adopt a much stricter principle of church-state separation—we might call them "religious separationists"—on the ground (again following Roger Williams) that any contact between state and church, even when intended to benefit religion, ends up corrupting and weakening it.

Other analysts emphasize the "Enlightenment" position, emphasizing that Jefferson, Madison (to a much lesser degree), and some other leaders in the founding generation were believers in rationality and were suspicious of traditional religious dogma and concerned about religious fanaticism and its effects on society. Proponents of this position tend to adopt a version of church-state separation that emphasizes keeping the public sphere secular and free from the extremes that religion can provoke. (We might call them "secular separationists.")

However, other analysts argue that the Religion Clauses reflect no substantive theory about how government should treat religion—but only a prudential judgment that the new federal government should not be involved in such matters. In this view, the religion provision was primarily a product of federalism: that government policy toward religion, whatever it might be, should be left to the states. These critics point to the fact that there was disagreement throughout the states in 1789 about how government should treat religion, but that in the brief congressional debates on the First Amendment none of these disputes was discussed in any detail or resolved. Thus, it is argued, the framers could have done no more than assign these matters to the states.

If this position is correct, then it is fruitless to try to find in the First Amendment some grand theoretical statement on religious freedom. Another consequence is that it may be awkward or even illogical to apply the Religion Clauses to restrict state governments (through incorporation in the Fourteenth Amendment), since under this view the clauses' sole rationale was to give states discretion to regulate religion. But this "federalism" view has been subjected to criticism. Substantive views about religious freedom did play some role in the development of religious freedom. Moreover, it is argued, matters may have changed dramatically by the time the Fourteenth Amendment was enacted in 1868: states by that time might have been seen as an equal threat, so that the rule disabling the federal government from regulating religion should now equally apply to them.

As was mentioned above, at the time the First Amendment was adopted, three New England states (Connecticut, Massachusetts, and New Hampshire) still maintained "establishments" in the sense of assessing taxes to pay for churches and ministers. (The presence of establishments at that time is one reason the "federalism" theorists argue that the founders could not have meant to disapprove establishments as a matter of principle.) But these religious taxes had been liberalized: in theory at least, the taxpayer could be exempted or could designate which denomination would receive his tax.

Finally, in the early 1800s, the system of religious assessments remaining in New England broke down because of a major rift within the dominant Congregational denomination. In Massachusetts especially, more and more local parishes and ministers in this period adopted Unitarian beliefs, rejecting the divinity of Jesus, and their conservative opponents began to rue the fact that the state government was giving support to such heretical views. The episode provides a good example of how increased religious pluralism undercuts establishment by making it impossible for one religious body to capture the government to its satisfaction. Religious assessments finally ended in Massachusetts in 1833.

D. THE NINETEENTH CENTURY: THE "DE FACTO" PROTESTANT ESTABLISHMENT AND THE ENACTMENT OF THE FOURTEENTH AMENDMENT

Neither the enactment of the federal First Amendment nor the end of state religious assessments, however, meant that governments in America stopped acting to favor the Christian religion. The 1800s saw the development or continuation of a host of government practices that supported a general, nondenominational Protestantism and that disfavored or restricted other views on religion. Together these practices created what has sometimes been called a "de facto" establishment of Protestant Christianity.

State laws prohibiting blasphemy—malicious attacks against God or Christianity—continued to be enforced for the first third of the 1800s. Chancellor Kent of New York sustained such a prosecution on the ground that "we are a Christian people, and the morality of the country is deeply engrafted upon Christianity." *People v. Ruggles* (N.Y.1811). The

Supreme Court and other courts indicated their approval of such laws on the ground that Christianity is "part of the common law of" the American states. *Vidal v. Girard's Executioners* (S.Ct.1844); *Updegraph v. Commonwealth* (Pa.1824). States also retained laws forbidding work or other activities on Sunday. Toward the end of the century, the Court recited a long list of religious utterances by American governments and concluded that "this is a Christian nation." *Holy Trinity Church v. United States* (S.Ct.1892). And as we have noted, the disqualification of non-Christians, or at least non-theists, from public office continued in many states well into the 1900s.

Prayers and readings of the Bible continued to be part of official ceremonies, particularly in the new public schools, which began to appear in the 1830s and 1840s. Indeed, the public schools were created in significant part to permit the education of children in Protestant values across denominational differences. The form of such exercises—readings from the Protestant (King James) Bible, prayers and readings without guidance from clergy—were objectionable to many Catholics, whose numbers in urban areas were growing rapidly because of immigration. Sometimes Catholic children were punished for refusing to participate in the exercises, and on a few occasions such disputes erupted into anti-Catholic riots (the most serious one in Philadelphia in 1844).

Christianity was prevalent in government activities because it was pervasive in 19th-century culture. The active churchgoing population mushroomed as a result of a series of religious revivals in the years around 1800, led by the Methodists and Baptists. These denominations had, of course, renounced reliance on the government for financial support; and the vitality of churches in general in these years is sometimes attributed to the fact that they no longer leaned on the government. (The famous clergyman Lyman Beecher, who had fought hard to preserve religious taxes in Connecticut, said later that disestablishment was the best thing that had happened to the churches.) But the Baptists and Methodists joined most other Christian bodies in continuing to affirm that government should explicitly promote and reflect general Christian teachings.

Constitutional commentators today draw different conclusions from the pervasive government promotion of Christianity in the 1800s. Some say that it confirms the fact that the framers of the First Amendment meant only to prohibit preferences for one Christian denomination, leaving government free to promote the general Christian or "Judeo–Christian" tradition. (Justice Joseph Story, in his 1833 commentaries on the Constitution, adopted this view, writing that the purpose of the Religion Clauses "was, not to countenance, much less to advance Mahometanism [i.e. Islam], or Judaism; but to exclude all rivalry among Christian sects.") Opponents of this reasoning respond that the Religion Clauses at that time still only applied to the federal government (as the Supreme Court made clear in *Permoli v. First Municipality of New Orleans* (S.Ct.1845)). The states were still constitutionally free to make their own policies on religion; it does not follow that once the states are restricted by the First Amendment, they can still promote general Christianity.

As a pervasive force in American culture, Christianity also deeply influenced political and social debates. The religious revivals spawned Christian reform movements for a host of causes, including temperance, education, relief for the poor, and the abolition of gambling and slavery. Defenders of slavery appealed to the Bible as well; and Abraham Lincoln could note in his Second Inaugural Address that both sides in the Civil War "read the same Bible, and pray to the same God." Lincoln's speeches, like many public discourses of the day, were laced with Biblical imagery.

The 19th century de facto Protestant establishment also produced one of the most sustained and successful efforts in American history to suppress a religious practice: the federal government's campaign to force the Mormon Church to renounce the custom of polygamy or plural marriage. The practice, engaged in by many of the church's leaders although not by the majority of Mormon men, was based at least in part on the church's interpretation of Old Testament scripture. Founded in upstate New York, the Mormon movement fled angry mobs in the Midwest and eventually, in 1847, trekked west to settle in a land that the United States would soon purchase and make the territory of

Utah. Within a few years, Congress responded to an aroused public opinion by explicitly making polygamy a crime. The Supreme Court upheld the application of the law to Mormons in *Reynolds v. United States* (S.Ct.1879).

The Mormon Church did not immediately renounce polygamy, however, and the government stepped up the pressure. It required all voters in Utah to swear that they did not belong to an organization that advocated polygamy; finally it ordered the dissolution of the Mormon Church and the confiscation of much of its property, including the new temple in Salt Lake City. The Supreme Court upheld both these actions on the ground that polygamy was a threat "to the spirit of Christianity and of the civilization which Christianity has produced in the western world." *Late Corporation of Latter–Day Saints v. United States* (S.Ct.1890) (upholding confiscation); see *Davis v. Beason* (S.Ct. 1890) (upholding oath requirement). Soon thereafter the church's president announced a new revelation freeing members from the duty of polygamy. The church's property was restored, Utah was admitted into the Union with a proviso that it must prohibit polygamy, and the Mormons set off on the way to becoming a socially mainstream and economically successful group.

The great constitutional change of the 1800s came with the enactment of the Thirteenth through Fifteenth Amendments immediately after the Civil War. The most important for these purposes is the Fourteenth Amendment (1868), which forbade any state to abridge the privilege and immunities of citizens of the United States, or to deny any person due process of law or the equal protection of the laws. Under this Amendment, particularly the due process provision, the Court since the 1940s has subjected state and local governments to the restrictions of the Bill of Rights, including the religion provision. However, debate still continues about whether the Amendment's drafters and ratifiers intended it to incorporate any or all of the Bill of Rights.

With respect to religious freedom, the incorporation debate is complicated by the episode of the Blaine Amendment, a proposed constitutional amendment that would have explicitly applied the Religion Clauses to the states, but which failed to pass Congress in 1875 because it lacked the necessary two-thirds vote in the Senate. Critics of incorporation assert that Congress never would even have considered such a proposal if it had decided just a few years earlier to apply the Religion Clauses to states. Defenders of incorporation respond that the Blaine Amendment may have been viewed as necessary even if incorporation had been intended by the Fourteenth Amendment, because the Supreme Court had (wrongly) eviscerated the Amendment in the interim in the *Slaughter–House Cases* (S.Ct.1873). Other defenders of incorporation argue that the Blaine Amendment failed not because it would have applied the religion provisions to states, but because it would have explicitly authorized (Protestant) Bible reading in public schools while forbidding any aid to "sectarian" (that is, Catholic) schools.

E. RELIGIOUS PLURALISM AND MODERN CHURCH–STATE RELATIONS

The last part of the 19th century brought great changes that eroded the Protestant dominance of American culture and public life. Continued immigration from central, southern, and eastern Europe dramatically increased the percentage of Catholics in the population and also produced significant Jewish communities, especially in the major cities. The cities themselves grew rapidly, drawing people from out of rural areas to a new kind of life where the church did not have nearly the influence that it exercised in small towns. Traditional religion was attacked by powerful new scientific and political ideas—most notably Darwinian evolution, which called into question the Biblical account of creation, and Marxian socialism, which dismissed religion as an "opiate" that kept the working classes contented in their oppression.

As a result of these factors, the United States by the early 1900s was becoming more and more pluralistic in religious matters and, at least among the influential professional and academic classes, more and more secularized.

One wing of Protestantism tried to adapt to these changes by accepting so-called historical criticism of the Bible, treating some orthodox doctrines as symbolic rather than literal, and interpreting the Christian message to condemn modern industrial conditions (the "Social Gospel"). The conservative wing opposed all these changes in the name of what it called the "fundamentals" of Christianity. However, the fundamentalists failed in their efforts to banish more liberal elements from their denominations. Moreover, after the 1925 Scopes trial in Tennessee, in which a biology teacher was prosecuted for teaching Darwinian evolution, fundamentalists were widely perceived as backward and anti-intellectual. Many fundamentalists retreated from involvement in public life or political matters, concentrating on creating their own schools and media outlets; they would not emerge again into politics for almost 50 years, but when they did it would be with a vengeance.

Meanwhile, the Supreme Court began to hold that religious freedom was constitutionally protected against the state as well as federal governments, thus extending constitutional restrictions to a much wider range of government actions. A major step came in the 1920s, when the Court struck down Nebraska law that prohibited any school from teaching a foreign language (as applied to religious and other private schools), and also struck down an Oregon law that prohibited parents from sending their children to anything other than a public school. *Meyer v. Nebraska* (S.Ct.1923); *Pierce v. Society of Sisters* (S.Ct.1925). Both laws had been enacted in a wave of sentiment against Catholic immigrants. The Court held that the laws violated the Fourteenth Amendment by depriving parents of liberty without due process of law. This liberty, the Court said, included the rights to worship God and to bring up children without unreasonable interference from the state.

Meyer and *Pierce* rested on the same "substantive" interpretation of the Due Process Clause that the Court had been using to strike down certain forms of economic regulation in the pre-New Deal years. However, by treating religious freedom as a fundamental liberty under the clause, the decisions paved the way for the Court to incorporate fully the First Amendment's religious freedom guarantees into the Fourteenth Amendment. The Court incorporated the two religion provisions in two decisions in the 1940s. *Cantwell v. Connecticut* (S.Ct.1940) (Free Exercise Clause); *Everson v. Board of Education* (S.Ct.1947) (Establishment Clause).

Cantwell, like most of the early decisions protecting religious activity from state and local laws, involved the activity of Jehovah's Witnesses. This aggressive sect did extensive street preaching and door-to-door solicitation in the 1930s and 1940s, making verbal attacks on the United States government and on organized religion, especially the Roman Catholic Church. Efforts by states and towns to restrict the Witnesses' activity led to 18 Supreme Court decisions between 1938 and 1953. More and more, the Court began to hold that regulations must give way in the face of the Witnesses' rights, both of free speech and free exercise of religion. Coming after the New Deal Court had begun deferring to government economic regulations, these decisions established speech and religion as among the "preferred freedoms" that required an unusually strong justification to restrict.

The 1950s saw a revival of sentiment for public, traditional religion, as parents began to raise the "baby boom" generation and the nation steeled itself for a conflict with Soviet Communism and its atheistic philosophy. But the religious mainstream that government sought to promote reflected the nation's increased pluralism: it had now expanded from Protestantism to include Catholicism and Judaism in a general "Judeo–Christian" tradition, as noted in Will Herberg's book *Protestant Catholic Jew* (1955). Congress amended the Pledge of Allegiance in 1954 to make "One nation, indivisible" read "One nation, under God, indivisible." Perhaps reflecting the national mood, the Supreme Court issued an opinion stating that "We are a religious people whose institutions presuppose a Supreme Being." *Zorach v. Clauson* (S.Ct.1952).

In the 1960s and 70s, however, under the Chief Justiceships of Earl Warren and Warren Burger, the Court rendered decisions that dramatically affected the pattern of interaction between state governments and religion. The Court struck down state-sponsored prayers and Bible readings in public schools, practices that had been widespread since the creation of public schools. *Engel v. Vitale* (S.Ct. 1962); *Abington School District v. Schempp* (S.Ct. 1963); see Chapter 4. Later, it struck down the provision of state aid to support teachers in religiously affiliated elementary and high schools. *Lemon v. Kurtzman* (S.Ct.1971); see Chapter 5. These decisions, and others following them, will be discussed in detail in later chapters; but for now suffice to say that, overall, they tended to reflect a fairly strong form of the principle of separation of church and state.

These decisions provoked intense, sharply divided reactions among commentators and the public. Some saw them as inevitable responses to the increasing pluralism of American religion, which made any government support for a single religious observance far too partial and exclusive of too many citizens. In this view, the Court was simply following the logic of the Religion Clauses to disapprove practices that had escaped scrutiny in the past because they were innocuous to most Christians.

Many people in the public, however, saw the decisions as both reflecting and increasing the trend of secularization in society, with government required to be entirely free of religious influences and religion confined to people's private lives. Among the latter group, the school prayer decisions were especially unpopular; but though opponents made several efforts to overturn the decisions by constitutional amendment in the 1960s, they failed in their efforts.

The school prayer decisions, together with other legal and cultural developments such as the declaration of abortion rights in *Roe v. Wade* (S.Ct.1973), galvanized the large population of conservative

Protestants who had been relatively inactive in political affairs since the 1920s. Beginning in the 1970s, groups such as the Moral Majority and, later, the Christian Coalition mobilized these voters to support conservative social policies: restrictions on abortion, resistance to homosexual rights, a return of organized prayer to the public schools, and so forth. This "Religious Right," joined by many conservative Catholics and a much smaller number of conservative Jews, played some role in helping elect Presidents Reagan and Bush.

The rise of the Religious Right prompted a new debate over the proper role of religion in American politics. Members of the movement were accused of trying to "impose their religious views" on others. They replied that in bringing their religious views to bear on politics, they were only doing what other Americans, and especially political liberals, had long done in campaigns such as the civil rights movement.

The rise of conservative religious activism also prompted a new debate about the meaning of the Religion Clauses. Among the promises of Republican presidential candidates was to appoint federal judges who would exercise "judicial restraint," which included greater deference to the majority's views concerning government and religion. The appointment of several justices by Republicans has indeed led the Court to retreat from a strong form of church-state separation in some areas, particularly by allowing more extensive government aid to religious organizations (see Chapter 5). However, as we will see, the current Court has also reaffirmed important parts of the 1960s and 1970s legacy, including the ban on state-sponsored prayer at public school events (see Chapter 4, discussing *Lee v. Weisman* (S.Ct.1992)).

Although the basic underlying principles of religious freedom are similar throughout American history, the debate has shifted ground in ways that reveal the increased pluralism in American religion, and thus the need to be aware of more potential impositions on minority religions. At the time of the founding, a general official prayer to God or even to Jesus was non-controversial to most Americans; today, however, such a prayer is constitutionally suspect. While even the radical Roger Williams supported legislating under the second five commandments (see *supra*), today scholars discuss seriously the issue whether laws may be based in any significant way on religious values. Justices and commentators debate whether these changes reflect a rejection of the historic approach to the state and religion, or whether they simply involve the application of settled principles of religious liberty to new circumstances brought on by our increasing pluralism in religious views.

CHAPTER THREE

FREE EXERCISE OF RELIGION

Overview

The constitutional guarantee against laws "prohibiting the free exercise" of religion raises questions that are, in some ways, more familiar than those raised by the prohibition on laws respecting an establishment of religion. The free exercise guarantee has analogies to the guarantees of freedom of speech and freedom of the press; all arise in situations where government prevents an individual or group from engaging in a constitutionally protected activity. (By contrast, the Establishment Clause may apply to certain government actions even when no individual or group is directly restricted in its own activity.)

The case law under the Free Exercise Clause has become fairly clear in recent years. Some of the governing rules are relatively uncontroversial: government may not interfere with religious belief, it may not restrict religious expression without meeting the strict standards of free speech law, and it may not restrict religiously motivated conduct in a discriminatory fashion. But the next rule is much more important and controversial: government may prohibit or restrict religiously motivated conduct if it does so under a law that generally applies to all citizens and does not single out religion. This last rule, announced in *Employment Division v. Smith* (S.Ct.1990), covers the most common kind of government action affecting religious exercise. Since the rule denies federal constitutional protection in a great many cases, claimants seeking broad free exercise rights have turned their attention to other sources of law, primarily to federal statutory protections and to state constitutions and statutes.

A. UNQUESTIONED PRINCIPLES OF FREE EXERCISE: FREEDOM OF BELIEF, FREEDOM OF EXPRESSION, AND NONDISCRIMINATION

1. Freedom of Belief

It is helpful to cover the less controversial rules first. To begin with, "the Free Exercise Clause categorically forbids government from regulating, prohibiting or rewarding religious beliefs as such." *McDaniel v. Paty* (S.Ct.1978). Seldom in recent history has an American government imposed a punishment or disability on a person solely because he held a certain religious belief or opinion, as opposed to engaging in a certain practice. During its campaign against Mormon polygamy in the late 1800s, the federal government did require voters in the Territory of Utah to swear that they were not a member of any organization that taught polygamy, and the Supreme Court upheld the requirement. *Davis v. Beason* (S.Ct.1890). But that result would likely be overturned today.

One regulation based on religious belief was common throughout much of American history: the requirement that public office holders swear a belief in God or in Jesus Christ. Such oaths were barred for federal government offices by the Religious Test Clause of Article VI. But that provision, although a little ambiguous, probably applies only to the federal government. Religious tests for state and local government offices are prohibited instead by the (incorporated) First Amendment Religion Clauses, under *Torcaso v. Watkins* (S.Ct.1961).

While *Torcaso* is now bedrock law, it does prompt one threshold question: which provision of the First Amendment protects the right **not** to believe or profess any religion? The Court listed some religions, such as Buddhism and Taoism, that do not believe in a deity and whose adherents therefore would be violating their beliefs by signing the oath. But imagine a person whose reason for refusing to swear is that she rejects all religion: can she claim a violation of her right to exercise religion freely? Possibly the Free Exercise Clause does protect the right not to follow religion as well to follow it—just as the Free Speech Clause has often been held to protect "the right not to speak." Alternatively, perhaps when a test oath for office is applied to a person who does not believe in any religion, it violates the Establishment Clause by imposing theistic religion. *Torcaso* did not differentiate between the two clauses, citing cases under both, and indeed here the two provisions seem to work in harmony.

2. Freedom of Expression

A second category of religious activity that un-questionably receives strong protection is religious expression and worship. This was not always so. The 17th-century English Puritan government of Oliver Cromwell did not require Catholics to convert but did ban celebration of the mass; in Franco's Spain, Protestants could meet privately but sometimes were forbidden to worship publicly or distribute literature. But speech and worship obviously are crucial aspects of religious life. Conversely, religious expression has been crucial in the development of America's tradition of freedom of speech. Religious sermons and tracts helped fuel both the American Revolution and the movement to abolish slavery. And much of the modern law of free speech was made in decisions involving the Jehovah's Witnesses in the 1940s and the religiously-inspired civil rights movement in the 1960s. As Justice Scalia has put it, "a free-speech clause without religion would be *Hamlet* without the prince." *Capitol Square Review and Advisory Board v. Pinette* (S.Ct.1995) (plurality opinion).

In the Jehovah's Witness and civil rights cases, the Court established freedom of speech, including religious speech, as a "preferred" constitutional right that could only be regulated based on a strong governmental need. See, e.g., *Murdock v. Pennsylvania* (S.Ct.1943) (striking down license tax applied to Jehovah's Witness street preachers); *West Virginia State Board of Education v. Barnette* (S.Ct.1943) (holding that Jehovah's Witness children could not be compelled to salute flag in violation of their consciences). In particular, speech generally cannot be prohibited or restricted because of its content unless the circumstances are exceptional. Government may place reasonable content-neutral restrictions on the "time, place, or manner" of speech, and these can be applied to religious speech as well; but it may not restrict religious speech because of its religious message or the effect that message will have on the audience.

A recent line of decisions has reaffirmed the equal right to religious speech in the face of a new contention: that the Establishment Clause requires the restriction of citizens' religious expression in public schools and other government institutions in order to preserve the separation of church and state. (These rulings are discussed in greater detail in Chapter 4.) The leading decision, *Widmar v. Vincent* (S.Ct.1981), held that a state university could not constitutionally forbid a student religious group to meet on campus when it allowed a wide range of other student groups to meet. By allowing meetings, the university had created a "public forum" (a concept drawn from other free speech cases) for student expression on its property. It could not exclude a group from the forum based on the religious content of the group's speech, absent a compelling governmental interest. No such interest was present, because permitting a private group to speak religiously would not be state sponsorship of religion.

This "equal access" principle has been extended to forbid the exclusion of religious speech in other circumstances. *Lamb's Chapel v. Center Moriches School District* (S.Ct.1993) (exclusion of church group from school classrooms open at night to community groups for social or civic purposes); *Pinette*, *supra* (exclusion of religious symbol from public square open to other symbols); *Rosenberger v. Rector of University of Virginia* (S.Ct.1995) (exclusion of religious magazine from university financial assistance available to other student publications).

The strong protection of religious expression, as well as of belief and worship, can be understood in terms of the underlying values of separation, equality, and religious liberty or choice. When the Court prohibits the state from restricting citizen's beliefs or expression simply because they are religious, the decision respects citizens' liberty and choice concerning religion. As *Widmar* emphasized, it also coincides with equality, since the government may not regulate the holding or expression of other, nonreligious views because of their content. (The government may enforce reasonable content-neutral restrictions, but these can also be applied to religious speech).

Finally, these protections generally serve to keep the state separate from religion. A very strict version of separation could require the exclusion of private religious speech from schools and other government institutions, to ensure that no one will attribute the speech to the government. But *Widmar* and later cases reject such a notion, partly because it clashes so strongly with religious equality and choice (see Chapter 4). Indeed, the exclusion of religious speech or worship would not avoid church-state entanglement either, because, as the *Widmar* majority noted in a footnote, the state would to define the term "religion" or "worship" and monitor group meetings for their content.

3. Discrimination Against Religious Conduct

In contrast, the law has afforded government more power when religious activity moves from belief or speech into conduct. Indeed, in its first major free exercise decision, allowing the criminal prosecution of members of the Mormon Church for engaging in polygamy or plural marriage, the Court seemed to allow unrestricted power over conduct: "Laws are made for the government of actions, and while they cannot interfere with mere religious belief and opinions, they may with practices." *Reynolds v. United States* (S.Ct.1879). The Court supported the distinction with statements of Thomas Jefferson, who wrote that "the legislative powers of the government reach actions only, and not opinions" and that "[one] has no natural right in opposition to his social duties."

To exclude religiously motivated conduct entirely from protection, however, appears inconsistent with the term "exercise of religion," which is broader than just belief or expression. Indeed, religious faiths typically demand that their adherents act or not act in certain ways. Perhaps significantly, the term "free exercise" replaced some earlier drafts of the First Amendment that had referred to "rights of conscience," a phrase that does not as directly connote conduct.

The modern Court has included conduct or practices within the Free Exercise Clause, but still has treated them differently, primarily on the ground that conduct can harm others in ways that belief and speech cannot. While "freedom to believe . . . is absolute," freedom to act, "in the nature of things . . . cannot be" but "remains subject to regulation for the protection of society." *Cantwell v. Connecticut* (S.Ct.1940). To quote Jefferson again, religious belief and speech, unlike conduct (in at least some forms), "neither breaks my leg nor picks my pocket."

However, it is clear that even conduct cannot be singled out for restriction simply because it is religiously motivated. An example of the Court's hostility to laws discriminating against religious practice is *McDaniel v. Paty* (S.Ct.1978), which unanimously struck down a Tennessee constitutional provision forbidding clergy from serving as state legislators. Although figures such as Jefferson and John Locke had supported the clergy disqualification in order to keep religious disputes out of politics, the Court found there was no persuasive reason to think that clergy would be "less careful of antiestablishment interests or less faithful to their oaths of civil office than their unordained counterparts." Justice Brennan, concurring, added that the Religion Clauses do not permit government to treat religious believers "as subversive of American ideals and therefore subject to unique disabilities."

A law singling out religious conduct for restriction is forbidden unless it is narrowly tailored to serve a compelling governmental interest, an extremely stringent test. *Church of the Lukumi Babalu Aye v. City of Hialeah* (S.Ct.1993). In *Lukumi*, the Court struck down several city ordinances that prohibited the ritual slaughter or sacrifice of animals, because the ordinances discriminated against the worship ceremonies of Santeria, an Afro–Caribbean religion. Even though the ordinances did not specifically mention the Santeria religion, their definition of animal sacrifice "exclude[d] almost all killings of animals except for religious sacrifice." For example, the city treated hunting, slaughter of animals for food, eradication of pests, and euthanasia as "necessary" forms of killing and therefore exempt from the ban.

Having found the ordinances discriminatory, the Court applied "the most rigorous scrutiny" and struck them down. The reasons asserted for the ban—protecting public health and preventing cruelty to animals—could not explain why it was directed solely against ritual sacrifice, since other killing of animals could raise these concerns as well.

Lukumi is important because it explicitly affirmed that the Court's previous ruling in *Employment Division v. Smith* (see part B–4), which eliminated almost all free exercise challenges to "generally applicable" laws, did not eliminate challenges to laws that are not generally applicable and that single out religiously motivated conduct. In addition, *Lukumi* indicates that the Court will examine a law carefully to see if it is discriminatory. Even though the Hialeah ordinances did not mention the Santeria religion on their face, the Court looked at their provisions and found them to be "gerrymandered" against the sect. A plurality of the Court also examined the record of City Council meetings at which the ordinances were enacted, and found in them clear expressions of hostility against the Santeria faith.

B. THE CONTROVERSIAL SITUATION: ACCOMMODATION OF RELIGIOUS CONDUCT AS AGAINST NONDIS-CRIMINATORY LAWS

Although the free exercise protections above are clear, the most important free exercise issue has prompted much more controversy. Seldom does government interfere with pure religious belief, or punish conduct only when it is religiously motivated. Far more common is the case where a law covering the general populace happens to conflict with the religious practices of some citizens. Legislators need not be intending to suppress religion; often they do not know about the effects a law has, or if they know, they are not concerned enough to change the law. Such potential conflicts are numerous because there is such a wide range of religious practices in pluralistic America, and because government now regulates so many areas of life. In such situations of conflict, religious believers have argued that the Free Exercise Clause entitles them to an "accommodation"—that is, an exemption from a law applicable to other conduct.

In terms of underlying values, protecting religious conduct against discriminatory laws promotes both religious liberty and equal treatment for religion, and thus (as seen above) it is widely accepted. But accommodating or exempting religious conduct in the face of general laws involves a tension. It still generally promotes religious liberty, since the believer faces just as much of a conflict with his religious duties from a general law as from a discriminatory one. But a religious exemption treats activity differently when it is motivated by religious versus nonreligious reasons, and if one follows the equality principle this could be seen as unjustified special treatment for religion. Thus to require free exercise exemptions has been much more controversial, and recently the Court has stopped requiring them at all.

In the decades before the 1960s, the Court rejected religious freedom claims raised against general laws. The Court's decisions expressed particular concern that such exemptions would undermine the laws and the government's authority. For example, in rejecting the Mormon defendants' claim that anti-polygamy laws could not apply to them because the practice was their religious duty, the Court warned that recognizing such a defense would "permit every citizen to become a law unto himself."

Reynolds, *supra*. And in holding that Jehovah's Witness schoolchildren could be compelled to salute the flag, the Court stated that "[t]he mere possession of religious convictions which contradict the relevant concerns of a political society does not relieve the citizen from the discharge of political responsibilities." *Minersville School District v. Gobitis* (S.Ct.1940). (*Gobitis* was overruled three years later in *West Virginia State Board of Education v. Barnette*, *supra*; but the Court focused more on the expressive than on the religious nature of the claim.)

As we will now see, for awhile the Court rejected *Reynolds* and required some accommodations for religious conduct against general laws. Recently, however, it returned to the *Reynolds* approach: the general rule now is that such accommodations are not constitutionally required. See *Employment Division v. Smith* (part B–4). In order to understand the issue, we need to follow the Court's back-and-forth decisions.

1. The Compelled Accommodations Test of *Sherbert* and *Yoder*

Despite the *Reynolds* precedent, the increasing status of religious exercise as a "preferred freedom" after World War II led the Court to hold that the Free Exercise Clause sometimes required exemptions from general laws. This doctrine was announced in *Sherbert v. Verner* (S.Ct.1963). Mrs. Sherbert, a Seventh–Day Adventist, was fired from her job because she would not work on Saturday, her sabbath day. For the same reason, she could not find another job. When she filed for state unemployment benefits, the state denied them on the ground that she had refused "without good cause" to accept "suitable work." The Supreme Court, however, reversed and required that she receive benefits.

The state placed a "substantial burden" on Mrs. Sherbert's religious exercise, the Court said, by denying benefits because of her unwillingness to work on Saturday. The state's rule put her to the choice of losing benefits or violating a "cardinal" tenet of her faith, and this "effectively penalized" her religiously motivated behavior. The imposition of such a burden could only be justified by a "compelling" or "paramount" interest, which the state could not show. There was no evidence that exempting Saturday worshippers would lead to fraudulent claims that would deplete the unemployment compensation fund; and even if there were, the state would have to show that there was no "alternative form of regulation" possible that would avoid infringing on free exercise.

Although *Sherbert* did not explore the question in detail, it appeared to embrace the doctrine of protecting religious practice even from general laws that apply to other reasons for acting. As the concurring and dissenting opinions observed, Mrs. Sherbert would have lost benefits had her reason for declining Saturday work been that she could not find a babysitter, or that she wanted to watch football on television.

Nine years later, the Court reaffirmed that a law "neutral on its face" nevertheless violated the Free Exercise Clause if it "unduly burden[ed]" religious exercise and was not supported by a "compelling" purpose. *Wisconsin v. Yoder* (S.Ct.1972). The Court held that state compulsory education laws could not be applied to parents in the Amish religious community who refused to send their children to school after age fourteen.

Under the first stage of the analysis—a significant burden on religion—the Court credited the Amish claim that schooling after that age would "expose[e the] children to worldly influences" contrary to the group's traditionalist beliefs, and would undermine the children's commitment to the insular Amish community. The Court emphasized the "high place" that America affords to "the values of parental direction of the religious upbringing and education of their children."

Under the second part of the test—a compelling or "overriding" governmental purpose—the Court said that although mandating education was an important purpose generally, the state's assertion had to be "searchingly examined" in the particular circumstances. The purpose of mandating education was to produce effective and self-reliant citizens. But the Amish had a 200–year-old tradition of training children for roles in their "separated agrarian" way of life, and they were "productive" citizens who generally rejected any form of public welfare support and therefore would not become "burdens on society." In addition, the state largely achieved its interests by requiring that the children attend school through eighth grade.

Yoder also raised an important issue about the protection of children's interests, but the majority partly sidestepped it. Justice Douglas, dissenting, argued that the children should be asked if they wanted to attend school, and if they did the parents' rights should give way; he argued that if children were "harnessed to the Amish way of life" by their parents and never exposed to other possibilities through education, they would lose their right "to be masters of their own destiny." The dissent thus raised the question to what extent the authority of the state should override the authority of the family in order to protect the child's autonomous decision-making. The majority replied that none of the children involved had actually expressed any such desire; in effect it deferred to the parents' authority unless the children raised an explicit objection.

Yoder suggested that the protection it was recognizing extended only to religious claims. It did cite the famous older decision holding that a law requiring children to be educated only in public schools violated the substantive "liberty" of parents found in the Due Process Clause (*Pierce v. Society of Sisters* (1925), discussed in Chapter 2). But *Yoder* also said that secular "philosophical and personal" views against public education—for example, a view that rejects mainstream social norms on the basis of the writings of Henry Thoreau—did not fall within the Religion Clauses and "may not be interposed as a barrier against reasonable state regulation of education."

2. Evaluating the Compelled Accommodations Doctrine

Sherbert and *Yoder* thus appeared to establish the rule that a substantial restriction on religious practice must be justified by a strong state interest, even if the restriction stems from a general law applicable to nonreligious conduct as well. As already noted, this rule seems to preserve the value of religious liberty, which can be infringed by a general law as much as by a discriminatory one. Arguably the rule also comports best with the term "free exercise," which itself appears most concerned with liberty. A general law applied to religion can be said to "prohibit[ ]" free exercise just as much as a discriminatory one. And as noted earlier, without exemptions the free exercise guarantee is relatively unimportant in practical terms today: government seldom singles out religion for prohibition, but the modern state with its extensive laws will often put some believer in a position of conflict between her religious duties and her legal duties.

However, the doctrine of constitutionally compelled exemptions or accommodations also raises complications and objections, many of which appeared in *Sherbert* and *Yoder* themselves. The major objections are: (a) religious exemptions unfairly favor religion over other reasons for acting; (b) the exemptions doctrine cannot be applied consistently or fairly by courts; and (c) the original understanding and history of the Free Exercise Clause do not support exemptions.

a. Favoritism for Religion?

Most importantly, if government were sometimes compelled to single out religious conduct for exemption, this seemed to conflict with language in Establishment Clause case law forbidding "any form of public aid or support for religion" and requiring "neutrality" toward religion (see, e.g., *Abington School Dist. v. Schempp* (S.Ct.1963), and other cases discussed in Chapter 4). Allowing a person freedom from the law simply on the basis of his religious tenets could be seen as aiding or favoring religion within the broad language of those decisions. Justice Stewart noted this "dilemma" in a concurring opinion in *Sherbert*. See also *Thomas v. Review Board* (S.Ct.1981) (Rehnquist, J., dissenting) (pointing out the "tension" between the two doctrines).

In terms of underlying values, the liberty-based rule of *Sherbert* and *Yoder* clashed with the notion of equal treatment between religion and other reasons for acting. Critics of the exemptions doctrine have asked why a religious motivation for acting should entitle one to an accommodation when other deeply-held motivations do not. Why, for example, should the Amish be able to keep their children from school when an equally sincere opponent of schools who follows Thoreau's teachings does not enjoy such a right? Or why should a person who refuses Saturday work in order to observe her Sabbath receive unemployment benefits when a mother who must stay home on Saturday to care for her children is denied benefits?

The clash between the free exercise and the broad doctrines of "no aid" was intensified in *Sherbert* and later cases involving unemployment compensation, because the Court required the state not merely to leave the believer alone but to pay her monetary benefits. One can defend these rulings, as *Sherbert* did, on the ground that withholding benefits can place just as much pressure on religious practices as flat out punishment can. To preserve religious freedom in the welfare state, the doctrine of "unconstitutional conditions" on state benefits must apply, as it does with other constitutional rights such as free speech (see, e.g., *Speiser v. Randall* (S.Ct.1958) (striking down statute conditioning tax benefit on claimant's willingness not to advocate overthrow of government)). However, this position was difficult to square with the Court's Establishment Clause rulings that prohibited financial aid to religious schools even when nonreligious private schools received them (see, e.g., *Lemon v. Kurtzman* (S.Ct.1971), discussed in Chapter 5). Those rulings effectively required that a school be nonreligious, or at least not "pervasively" religious, in order to receive benefits.

There were three possible ways to handle such conflicts. One is to hold that many or all accommodations or exemptions of religiously motivated conduct violate the Establishment Clause by favoring religion. This would make it a constitutional requirement for government to give facially equal treatment between religion and other reasons for acting. The Court has occasionally struck down an exemption for religious conduct because it unduly favors religion over non-religion (see part D below). But it has never held that all exemptions for religious practice are forbidden.

Second, it could be held that although religious exemptions are not constitutionally forbidden, the difficulties just mentioned also mean that they are not constitutionally required. Justice Harlan took this position in his dissenting opinion in *Sherbert*. Essentially, it says that because of the conflict between religious liberty and equal treatment, government is free to take either course, applying the general law or exempting religious conduct. As we will see, the Court majority has now adopted this position. It has the disadvantage, however, of tending to offer protection only to faiths that are numerically powerful or that are sufficiently adept in the political process to secure an exemption.

Finally, one could adhere to *Sherbert*, *Yoder*, and the religious liberty value, and conclude that religious accommodations are constitutionally required and are not a form of government aid or favoritism for religion. As one later decision put it, the government does not unconstitutionally advance religion "simply because it **allows** churches to advance religion" themselves by exempting them from regulation. *Corporation of Presiding Bishop v. Amos* (S.Ct. 1987) (emphasis in original) (upholding a statutory accommodation, though not holding that it was constitutionally compelled).

Defenders of compelled accommodations point out that the Free Exercise Clause singles out religious conduct for protection; thus, they reason, there is nothing anomalous about religious exemptions. Moreover, they argue, religious claims are indeed different from others. Religious believers, they say, tend to feel their motivations especially deeply, and to be especially pained, and resistant, when the state prevents them from following their conscience. Opponents of accommodation, however, argue that in many instances, religious beliefs are no more deeply held or sensitive than other conscientious beliefs. They also argue that the text of the Free Exercise Clause does not have to be read to require religious exemptions; the bar on "law[s] ... prohibit[ing] free exercise" it could be read simply to bar laws that single out religion by their terms.

Religious accommodations have also been defended on the ground that religious believers assert a duty to a power higher than the state—to a personal God or some ultimate reality. If the state rejects such claims, it may appear to be asserting a kind of ultimate authority that is disturbing. Defenders of accommodation, most notably Professor Michael McConnell, argue that the founding generation believed in this primacy of religious duties (see subsection (b) *infra*).

The argument that religious beliefs have a special status has undoubtedly played a major role in the development of religious freedom. But it also raises questions. Does this argument imply that accommodations of religion must rely on the premise that there is a God? If so, does the exemptions doctrine involve the state adopting a particular religious belief? Adopting such a belief arguably violates the Establishment Clause if that clause is held to require government to be neutral toward religion (at least under some broad understandings of "neutrality"). Some defenders of accommodation reply that the government is not required to be indifferent to religion, because religion is a positive social good whose free exercise should be encouraged.

While defenders of accommodation call for special protection of religiously-derived conduct, they typically assert that religious speech should receive only the same protection as other forms of speech. They agree that the government must give equal treatment to the expression of various viewpoints; but they argue that with respect to conduct, there is a right of accommodation for religious conduct that is based in the Free Exercise Clause and in the theory of duties to a higher power. Opponents of accommodation question this distinction between conduct and ideas, arguing that when government exempts conduct stemming from religious reasons but not conduct stemming from other beliefs, it still favors religious ideas in violation of the First Amendment rule of content neutrality.

In sum, religious exemptions are often defended under a liberty or choice-based analysis. Exempting a religious believer from a law does not compel anyone else to practice religion. In most cases, it has been argued, exemptions do not even induce or encourage others to choose religious practice. For example, no one will be tempted to become a Jehovah's Witness in order to be able to refuse a court-ordered blood transfusion in an emergency, or tempted to adopt the Amish faith in order to avoid sending his children to schools. Rather, exemptions protect people and groups who already wish to practice religion from having that choice forbidden or discouraged by government action. (This analysis is consistent with a different understanding of neutrality, which has been called "substantive" neutrality, discussed in Chapter 1.)

However, there are situations in which a religious exemption might make a practice so attractive that people would be tempted to convert (or claim to convert) in order to secure the exemption. For example, certain tax exemptions solely for religious organizations might attract people to join religious pursuits in order to gain a financial advantage. In such cases, where a practice coincided strongly with self-interest, even advocates of the religious choice value (or substantive neutrality) might decline to recognize an exemption.

It should also be noted even if constitutionally compelled accommodations produce unequal treatment between religion and non-religion, they do serve a different equality value: that of equal treatment for all religions, in particular for minority faiths and those lacking political power. Powerful or widely-followed faiths can already secure accommodations in the legislative process: for example, the government already accommodates Christianity by closing public schools and offices on Sundays. Judicially declared exemptions can ensure that minority faiths receive similar accommodation.

Nevertheless, it remains true that the exemptions doctrine treats religious conduct differently from other conduct. Some observers have suggested that the conflict between religious liberty and equality could be resolved by extending accommodations to conduct stemming from any deeply-held conscientious belief, not just from religious beliefs. To accomplish this, the definition of "religion" in the Free Exercise Clause would have to be broadened to include all deeply-held conscientious beliefs. The Supreme Court did expand the term in such a way in cases involving exemptions from the military draft for conscientious objectors to war—although these decisions interpreted the language of the exemption statute, not the Constitution. (For more detailed discussion, see Chapter 7, "The Definition of Religion").

This proposed solution, however, faces its own difficulties. Extending exemptions to any seriously-held belief would more severely hamper the government than would religious exemptions alone. Moreover, if all conscientious beliefs are "religion" for free exercise purposes, it seems the same would be true for non-establishment purposes: and would this paralyze government by forbidding it to promote virtually any serious moral outlook? Finally, it may be notable that the framers rejected earlier drafts of the First Amendment that protected the rights of "conscience" in favor of the current language concerning "religion." (See Chapters 2 and 7 for further discussion.)

b. *The Original Understanding*

Neither the decisions embracing the compelled exemptions doctrine (*Sherbert* and *Yoder*) nor the later decision rejecting it (*Employment Division v. Smith*) discussed the original understanding of the Free Exercise Clause. But recently the historical record on compelled exemptions was vigorously debated in the concurring and dissenting opinions in *City of Boerne v. Flores* (S.Ct.1997), where the Court invalidated Congress's attempt to restore the compelled exemptions rule by statute (see part C–2 below).

Justice O'Connor, in a dissenting opinion arguing for compelled accommodations, referred to many state constitutions enacted in the late 1700s that explicitly said religious practice should remain unrestricted unless it disturbed the "peace or safety" of the state—suggesting that peaceful religious practice could not be restricted even by a generally applicable law. This wide consensus, she argued, was likely embodied in the First Amendment as well. In addition, state and colonial legislatures and the Continental Congress had granted exemptions to citizens who objected to oath requirements, military conscription, and religious assessments. Such exemptions, it can be argued, reflected the belief that religious duties were uniquely important—a belief held widely in the founding generation, and particularly by the Baptists and other dissenting groups who played such a prominent role in the campaign for religious liberty. For example, James Madison's "Memorial and Remonstrance Against Religious Assessments" begins with the contention that duties to the Creator are "precedent, both in order of time and in degree of obligation, to the claims of civil society."

But Justice Scalia, concurring in *Boerne*, countered that the "peace or safety" limitations in state constitutions meant that religious practice could be prohibited by general laws. He argued that there were almost no examples of courts in the founding generation requiring an exemption from a general law because of religious conscience. The grant of exemptions by the legislature, he added, did not prove that the exemptions were viewed as constitutionally compelled.

As both sides in the debate concede, there are difficulties with drawing conclusions about exemptions today based on specific government actions in the late 1700s. For several reasons, that generation may not have focused much attention on the question of constitutionally compelled accommodations from general laws. Nearly all citizens believed in general Protestant Christian standards of conduct that were embodied in the laws; government did not regulate society as extensively as today; and courts did not regularly review laws to assess their constitutionality. (Some scholars suggest that the history of the Fourteenth Amendment, a period closer to today's, provides better guidance and may support the notion that religious practice must sometimes be accommodated. But the Court has never examined this period in any detail.)

c. Applying the Doctrine Consistently

The compelled accommodations doctrine also presented difficulties in sorting out proper cases for exemption from improper ones. It is agreed that in some cases religious duties must be overridden by social duties or the rights of others; for example, no one can assert a free exercise right to practice human sacrifice. But just what is the standard for deciding such issues: in *Sherbert* and *Yoder*'s terms, what is a compelling or overriding purpose?

Distinguishing valid from invalid claims can be difficult, as both *Sherbert* and *Yoder* exemplify. *Sherbert* said there was no showing that persons claiming an inability to work on Saturday were draining the unemployment fund, but it suggested that the state would not be compelled to provide benefits to a person whose religion forbade her to work at all. One can readily see a difference between the two cases; but just where is the line between them, and what if the state made a reasonable prediction that there would be many Saturday-sabbath claimants? Likewise, *Yoder* said that the general importance of education was not decisive there because the Amish had a record of successful vocational education and community productivity. But to distinguish the Amish from other possible claimants, the Court had to engage in an intensive, very case-specific examination of Amish practices, without setting down a clear rule for other cases.

Some critics claim that the doctrine of compelled exemptions inevitably will be too case-specific, will not be sufficiently guided by general principles, and will discriminate in favor of more familiar faiths such as the Amish. Defenders of exemptions say that whatever uncertainty the case-specific approach causes is better than freeing the government from any duty to accommodate religious conscience at all. They add that the legislature alone is likely to be even less principled and fair in accommodating different religious claims than are the courts.

3. The Application and Decline of the Compelled Accommodations Doctrine

Before we discuss the demise of the *Sherbert/Yoder* compelled accommodations doctrine in *Employment Division v. Smith*, it is worth examining how the doctrine was applied in Court decisions during its lifetime. Even though under the *Smith* decision exemptions are now seldom required by the Free Exercise Clause, they may still be required by other sources of law, including federal statutes and state constitutions or statutes (see part C). In such cases, courts may be influenced by how the Supreme Court applied the exemptions doctrine after *Yoder* and before *Smith*. During that period, the Court ruled on both parts of the test: (1) Has the government significantly burdened a sincerely-motivated religious practice? (2) Is the burden justified by a strong or compelling interest? In general, the Court applied both parts with less and less vigor.

a. *Significant Burdens on Sincere Religious Exercise*

This was the threshold that triggered the government's duty to give a strong reason for a law. The Court increasingly raised this barrier so as to free the government from having to provide such justification.

First, we should note that the Court has been quite lenient in accepting a claimant's description of his religious beliefs and his assertion that they are sincere. It is difficult for a court to question a person's claim as to the nature or sincerity of his religious beliefs. Although some such inquiry must be done to prevent fraudulent claims, judges must always be careful not to impose too limited ideals of what constitutes religion.

A series of unemployment decisions following *Sherbert* expanded the category of cognizable religious claims, deferring more and more to the individual's characterization of his beliefs. The Court held that a Jehovah's Witness could not be denied benefits because he refused to work in a factory that made components for army tanks, even though the man could not clearly articulate the doctrinal basis for his refusal and other Jehovah's Witnesses saw no problem in working there. *Thomas v. Review Board* (S.Ct.1981). The justices refused to question Thomas's understanding of his faith, noting that "[c]ourts are not arbiters of scriptural interpretation." A later decision extended benefits to a worker who claimed he could not take Sunday work because he was a Christian even though he was not a member of any congregation or denomination. *Frazee v. Illinois Department of Employment Security* (S.Ct.1989). The Court acknowledged that such membership would make it easier to confirm that a claimant's beliefs were sincerely religious; but it refused to adopt membership as a requirement.

It is also clear that a court may not evaluate the truth of a religious doctrine in deciding whether it is protected. The Court has stated that "[h]eresy trials are foreign to our Constitution. Men may believe what they cannot prove. They may not be put to the proof of their religious doctrines or beliefs." *United States v. Ballard* (S.Ct.1944). In *Ballard*, the leaders of a new religious sect called the "I Am" movement were prosecuted for mail fraud for making assertions, which they allegedly knew were false, that they were divine messengers and had healed diseases. Interestingly, the defendants wanted to try the issue of whether some of their representations were actually false (the prosecution argued that it was enough that the defendants disbelieved their representations). The Supreme Court ruled that the issue of truth could not be put to the jury. This deprived the defendants of an issue, but it also seemed to mean that there could be no prosecution for some of the sect's assertions, for example that they were divine messengers.

Other assertions by the sect, however, would seem to concern worldly rather than other-worldly matters and thus triable issues of truth: for example, whether a particular sick person's symptoms had actually disappeared or not. Religious leaders can certainly be held liable for fraudulent statements of earthly fact. See, e.g., *United States v. Bakker* (4th Cir.1991) (criminal fraud conviction for misstating how contributions to religious ministry were being used; conviction upheld although sentence overturned).

The generally lenient approach to religious sincerity and the interpretation of religious claims is supported by strong reasons, but it also has caused concern to judges and commentators. Such leniency makes it harder to screen out insincere or marginal claims where the government should not have to show a strong reason for regulation. Must a court treat as legitimate, and give presumptive protection to, a person's claim that his religion forbids him from paying any taxes, or requires him to engage in prostitution, or requires that he appear in a chicken costume in court?

Perhaps responding to such concerns, the Court began developing other threshold barriers that kept the compelling interest test from being triggered. The test was held not to apply in the military, so that an Orthodox Jewish officer in the Air Force could be forbidden to wear his yarmulke even if the rule against headgear did not create a "clear danger" to military discipline or performance. *Goldman v. Weinberger* (S.Ct.1986). (In an example of political accommodation of religious exercise, Congress reacted to *Goldman* by passing a law protecting such religious dress in the Air Force.) For similar reasons of order and discipline, prison regulations that prevent inmates' religious exercise need only meet the deferential standard of being reasonably related to a legitimate interest. *O'Lone v. Estate of Shabazz* (S.Ct.1987).

More importantly, the Court in several decisions held that government had not imposed a "constitutionally significant burden" on religious exercise unless it had forced or pressured the claimant to violate a tenet of her religion—either by mandating conduct forbidden by the faith or by forbidding conduct mandated by the faith. In *Lyng v. Northwest Indian Cemetery Protective Association* (S.Ct. 1988), the Court held that the federal government had not inflicted any coercion on Native American worshippers by building a logging road through a forest on government-owned land which the Native Americans had long held sacred and used for worship. The majority accepted that the destruction of the site would have "devastating effects" on the Indians' ability to practice their religion. But it said that the government had not burdened the worshippers in a constitutional sense, because it had not put any pressure or penalty on them but had simply managed its land in a way that made their practices more difficult. Thus the government need not come forward with a strong justification for building the road (which, in fact, a Forest Service report had suggested was not particularly necessary). See also

Bowen v. Roy (S.Ct.1986) (holding that the government imposed no restriction on Native American religious believers by assigning Native American girl a social security number).

In holding that the government could make religious practice much more difficult as long as it did not directly forbid or restrict it, *Lyng* recalled the earlier decision of *Braunfeld v. Brown* (S.Ct.1961). There the Court rejected the claims of several observant Jewish merchants to be exempt from state laws requiring that businesses close on Sundays. The merchants' beliefs prohibited them from opening their shops on Saturday, while non-Jews could conduct business, and the closing laws then prohibited them from making up their lost business by opening on Sunday. *Braunfeld* held that the burden inflicted by the laws was merely "indirect" because they did not actually make the merchants' religious practices unlawful, but only more difficult and expensive.

Lyng regarded the government action as noncoercive. Shortly thereafter the Court upheld a state sales tax as applied to the sales of Bibles and religious tracts because the imposition of the tax, though certainly coercive, did not conflict with any mandatory tenets of the religious group. *Jimmy Swaggart Ministries v. Board of Equalization* (S.Ct. 1990). The evangelistic ministry that sold the books would lose money for its activities, but it could not show any tenet that prohibited it from paying the tax. Again, therefore, there was no constitutionally significant burden and the state need not show a strong interest in applying the tax.

By requiring that a free exercise claimant show he was forced to violate a command or prohibition of his faith, *Swaggart* significantly limited challenges to general laws. Supporters of broad free exercise exemptions say that *Swaggart* is inconsistent with the nature of religious activity, which often does not involve specific religious commands or prohibitions but is nevertheless deeply motivated by religious commitment. Courts applying the *Swaggart* rule have denied free exercise protection to claims involving the pursuit of the ministry as a career, or the building of a church in a particular location, on the ground that no specific tenet commanded such activities. See, e.g., *Witters v. State Commission for the Blind* (Wash.1989) (upholding denial of state aid to student because he was studying for ministry); *Cornerstone Bible Church v. City of Hastings* (8th Cir.1991) (rejecting free exercise challenge to zoning law excluding churches from downtown area, although sustaining other challenges).

In these decisions, the Court often seemed concerned about the effects of the compelled exemptions doctrine on government's ability to operate. *Lyng*, for example, expressed worry about interfering too greatly with the government's ability to manage its land—perhaps not just from the particular claim of Native Americans, but from the multiplicity of claims, possibly conflicting, that might have to be recognized. As part B–4 discusses, this attitude came to fruition with the rejection of the compelling interest test altogether in *Employment Division v. Smith*.

b. Compelling Interest

Narrowing the concept of burdens was the major way that the Court narrowed the government's duty to accommodate religious conduct. But the Court also found certain interests "compelling" so as to override free exercise claims. The compelling interest test in constitutional law began in the areas of regulation of speech and discrimination against racial minorities, where it almost always has led to the striking down of a law. But perhaps because the courts lost confidence in the compelled religious exemptions doctrine, they were willing to label a number of state interests as compelling in situations where religious conduct was burdened by general laws.

Most notably, in *United States v. Lee* (S.Ct.1982), the Supreme Court held that the federal government had a compelling interest in forcing Amish tradesmen to pay social security taxes as employers, even though the Amish objected on religious grounds because they believe in caring for their own needy. The Court said that allowing any exemptions from the social security system would logically lead to other exemptions and undermine the system's soundness. Indeed, the Court warned, allowing objectors to withhold social security taxes would logically mean also allowing people who objected to a particular part of the government budget (the military, for example) to withhold that percentage of their income taxes.

Although the *Lee* Court claimed to be applying the test of *Yoder*, it did not do so with much vigor. That earlier decision said that courts must examine the government's asserted need not at the most general level (for example, the need to have an educated population), but in the specific circumstances (the need to force Amish children to go to two years of high school). If *Lee* had followed this approach, it would likely have noted (as *Yoder* did) that the Amish care for their own and accept no social security or other government benefits themselves. The claimants in *Lee* employed only other Amish, so their nonpayment would not affect people outside the community. In general, exemptions from taxation might raise the danger of encouraging many other self-interested claims. But as Justice Stevens pointed out, an exemption for such unusual claimants as the Amish could be distinguished from, and so need not lead to, other tax exemptions. (Stevens concurred in denying the Amish claim because he opposes free exercise exemptions in all cases.)

The Court also found an overriding state interest (perhaps more defensibly) in *Bob Jones University v. United States* (S.Ct.1983), which upheld the IRS's withdrawal of tax-exempt status from private schools that practiced racial discrimination in admissions or in forbidding interracial dating among students. The IRS had ruled that such schools did not serve charitable purposes because their practices violated fundamental public policy. After suggesting that the loss of tax exemption was not a serious burden, the Court found the interest in "denying public support to racial discrimination in education" to be compelling, given the "stress and anguish" caused by state-sponsored race discrimination throughout American history.

Although the Court's reasoning was rather conclusory, two features that make a strong case for government regulation were present in *Bob Jones*. First, the underlying goal—avoiding state support for racial discrimination—was very important in view of the legacy of state-imposed slavery and segregation. One might ask, however, whether this goal would really be threatened by exempting a few schools that practiced segregation on religious grounds. Moreover, at least with respect to the policy on interracial student dating, the only persons affected would be those who voluntarily submitted to such rules by attending Bob Jones University.

Here the second feature comes in: allowing a religious exemption to some schools might encourage many others to practice racial discrimination in the name of religion and claim a similar exemption. If racism is still a potent force in American life, as many argue, then a significant number of schools might want to be able to follow discriminatory policies. They might seek strategically to cast their policies in religious terms; and as was mentioned above, it can be difficult to separate the sincere claims from the false ones.

These two features—(1) an especially important underlying public purpose and (2) a danger of encouraging many "strategic" claims that together would undermine that purpose—might also explain why the Court earlier declined to find a constitutional right for military conscientious objectors who opposed only particular wars rather than all wars (*Gillette v. United States* (S.Ct.1971)). Congress had already exempted those who opposed war in any form; but the Court found that it would be much harder for draft boards to make "fair, evenhanded, and uniform" evaluations of selective objectors. Their opposition by its nature might apply to only parts of a war, might change with new events, and might be difficult to distinguish from merely prudential concerns. These concerns, together with the importance of raising armies in the first place, were "substantial government interests" that justified the denial of selective conscientious objection claims.

If the compelling interest or heightened scrutiny test still applies in some cases (for example, under a state constitution), what other purposes might be important enough to satisfy it?

Courts have been most inclined to override religious claims when the religious conduct imposes direct harms to the person or property of others, as in the case of a religiously sanctioned human sacrifice. However, what if the affected person is a consenting adult? *State v. Pack* (Tenn.1975), for example, upheld an injunction against the holding of live poisonous snakes in certain Pentecostal worship services, even when no children were present. Applying the compelling interest test (although under the Tennessee state constitution), the court held that the state "has the right to guard against the creation of unnecessary widows and orphans" and maintain a "robust, taxpaying citizenry capable of self-support and of bearing arms."

This reasoning could be questioned. To be sure, "no man is an island." The believer who injures or kills herself may leave family members without support, and particularly in the welfare state such burdens are often assumed by society. But taken to its logical conclusion, such reasoning means that any aspect of a religious believer's health is a matter of state concern, which would leave little room for free exercise.

Cases of religiously motivated discrimination, such as *Bob Jones*, also raise questions about what is a compelling interest. Consider other such situations: a conservative church refuses to hire a woman minister or priest, a religious college refuses to recognize a gay and lesbian students' group, a landlord refuses to rent to an unmarried couple. In all these cases, the religious believer could be said to be inflicting direct harm on others. But there are important counter-arguments as well. In many cases the only people directly affected by the religiously based discrimination are those who have freely joined the community and therefore, arguably, submitted to its rules.

Can eradicating these other forms of discrimination be said to be a compelling goal, in the way that eradicating race discrimination is, and therefore override religious freedom? Some courts have said yes. *Gay Rights Coalition v. Georgetown University* (D.C.App.1987) (requiring college to subsidize and provide facilities to gay students' group but not to endorse it); *Smith v. Fair Employment and Housing Commission* (Cal.1996) (forbidding discrimination by religious landlord against unmarried couple). But other courts have questioned whether protecting homosexual or premarital sex can be a compelling goal, since such activities are still disapproved by many and in some cases are even illegal. *Attorney General v. Desilets* (Mass.1994).

Finally, some situations seem to involve not direct harms to specific persons, but rather more diffuse harms spread throughout society. Nevertheless, many courts found compelling regulatory needs in these circumstances, reasoning that granting one exemption would entail granting many and thus creating a serious regulatory gap. See, e.g., *Catholic High School Association v. Culvert* (2d Cir.1985) (applying labor laws to religious schools justified by interest in "industrial peace"); *New Life Baptist Church Academy v. Town of East Longmeadow* (1st Cir.1989) (detailed regulation of religious schools justified by state interest in educated citizens). Again, such decisions indicated that courts were not enforcing the compelled exemptions doctrine with much vigor.

4. The End of Compelled Accommodations: *Employment Division v. Smith*

Because of decisions such as *Lyng*, *Jimmy Swaggart*, and *Lee*, free exercise rights against general laws shrank considerably by the late 1980s. But the Court took a dramatic further step in *Employment Division v. Smith* (1990), eliminating the doctrine of compelled accommodations almost entirely. Two privately-employed drug rehabilitation counselors were fired from their jobs because they had ingested peyote, a hallucinogenic drug, for sacramental purposes at a ceremony of the Native American Church, of which they were members. The state of Oregon denied them unemployment benefits on the ground that they had been fired for work-related misconduct.

In court, the state argued that its criminal law against peyote use constituted a compelling reason for denying benefits under *Sherbert v. Verner* and *Wisconsin v. Yoder*. That assertion might present a close question. Justice O'Connor, concurring in the result in *Smith*, argued that the interest in combatting illegal, dangerous drugs was compelling. But Justice Blackmun, dissenting, pointed out that many states and the federal government exempted ritual peyote use, that the drug was generally used at controlled services of the Native American Church, and that ingesting it is an unpleasant experience that is unlikely to attract anyone other than sincere religious believers. The Court's majority brushed by the narrow issue of whether there was a compelling interest on these facts.

Instead the Court, in an opinion by Justice Scalia, reached out and held that the Free Exercise Clause poses no barrier to "neutral laws of general applicability," no matter how severely they infringe on religiously motivated behavior. So long as the government prohibits a certain practice generally, it does not have to give a compelling reason (and probably not any reason) for applying the prohibition to religious practice. Thus, the arguments about whether Native Americans' peyote use was really dangerous had no legal relevance; the state could punish it under a general law.

By holding that religious conduct could be prohibited pursuant to a neutrally and generally applicable law, *Smith* chose the principle of equal treatment between religion and non-religion over that of religious liberty. The majority essentially gave two reasons for doing so: precedent and judicial restraint.

a. Precedent

The Court argued that numerous decisions since the polygamy case (*Reynolds*) had rejected free exercise claims against general laws, so that the no-exemptions approach was "in accord with the vast majority of our precedents." The Court was right that recent decisions had been rejecting free exercise claims, but to rely on precedent it also had to distinguish *Sherbert* and *Yoder* themselves. It did so by announcing two exceptions to its general rule, exceptions where the compelling interest test apparently would still apply.

Yoder and several other cases were distinguished on the ground that they involved the Free Exercise Clause not alone, but "in conjunction with other constitutional protections." For example, the Court said, the decisions protecting street activity by Jehovah's Witnesses involved freedom of speech or press in conjunction with free exercise. In *Yoder*, the so-called "hybrid" constitutional claim was free exercise conjoined with "the right of parents ... to direct the educational upbringing of their children." (To read *Yoder* this way, as involving general parental rights, is questionable. That decision had stated that a parental claim "may not be interposed as a barrier to reasonable state regulation of education if it is based on purely secular considerations.")

Sherbert was distinguished on the ground that the unemployment eligibility statute was not really a general law with no exceptions. Instead, the standard of "good cause" for refusing available work "lent itself to individualized governmental assessment of the reasons for the relevant conduct." When "the state has in place a system of individual exemptions"—for example, when some reasons for refusing work would constitute good cause—"it may not refuse to extend that system to cases of 'religious hardship' without compelling reason."

These exceptions for "hybrid rights" and "individualized assessments" seem to have appeared in *Smith* mostly to avoid overruling any previous decision, and some courts have read them narrowly. See, e.g., *Salvation Army v. Department of Community Affairs* (3d Cir.1990). Moreover, the hybrid rights category is in some ways difficult to understand. If the other constitutional right (speech, association, property) is valid on its own, it is unclear what the free exercise interest adds; but if the other is not valid, it is unclear why two invalid constitutional claims should add up to a valid one.

Nevertheless, if the exceptions to *Smith*'s equal treatment rule were read broadly, they might preserve a fair number of free exercise challenges to general laws. A free exercise claimant can often put his claim under some other constitutional right as well. Many religious practices, from worship to styles of dress or grooming, can be seen as forms of expression; the use of church property could implicate the guarantee against takings of private property without compensation; and so on. Moreover, most laws have some exemptions in them (often for small businesses, or for powerful lobbies): if religious claimants must be exempted whenever any others are, they will be exempted often. It is unclear whether the Court will respond to such arguments by qualifying *Smith* and continuing to apply heightened scrutiny often.

The hybrid First Amendment rights of speech and association do seem particularly likely to protect religious groups from general laws in one recurring area of dispute: the hiring and treatment of clergy or other persons who speak publicly for the group. General laws against discrimination based on sex or sexual orientation conflict with some churches' tenets about who can serve as clergy or occupy other positions of leadership. One potential basis, among others, for churches to protect their autonomy in this area is that the clergy speak for the church, so that the church has a strong expressive interest in their selection.

b. Judicial Restraint

The most important argument in *Smith* was the majority's concern about the institutional role of judges. Justice Scalia's opinion essentially said that judicially mandated exemptions from general laws create an unacceptable dilemma. On one hand, if courts declared exemptions in many cases—that is, if the compelling interest test were applied strictly—the result would be "courting anarchy," in effect "permit[ting] every citizen to become a law unto himself." *Id.* (quoting *Reynolds v. United States*). This was a particular danger "[p]recisely because we are a cosmopolitan nation made up of people of almost every conceivable religious preference": the greater the variety of religious practices, the more exceptions would multiply. (A response might be that the greater variety of religious beliefs, the more also an unbending application of the law will create conflicts with conscience.)

But the Court also found unacceptable the suggestion that judges could apply a more moderate test for exemptions, "weigh[ing] the social importance of all law against the centrality of all religious beliefs." The Court indicated that weighing the importance of a law is not a judicial function for which there are principled legal standards, but rather a political judgment that should be made by electorally accountable officials. And on the "burden" side of the ledger, the Court argued that judges could not limit the compelling interest test to cases where the prohibited conduct is "central" to the claimant's religion. "It is not within the judicial ken to question the centrality of particular beliefs or practices to a faith, or the validity of particular litigants' interpretation of those creeds."

Thus *Smith* can be seen as the product of two interacting notions of judicial restraint. The first is deference to legislative and administrative decisions, reflected in the argument that widespread exemptions would "court anarchy." The second is a preference for formal rules, such as *Smith*'s equal-treatment rule, over "balancing" tests, such as the *Sherbert-Yoder* approach. The latter assertedly give judges too much discretion to reach preferred results in particular cases, and they fail to give the kind of guidance that the rule of law demands.

That *Smith* is based in judicial restraint is supported by the fact that it did not adopt one of the arguments against exemptions that was noted above (part B–2). The Court did not hold that accommodating religious conduct against a general law establishes religion by favoring it over other activities. The majority opinion did at one point call the free exercise exemption a "constitutional anomaly." But it later suggested that it is "permitted, or even ... desirable," for legislatures and other politically accountable bodies to exempt religious practice from general laws. (The issue of how far such legislative accommodations are permitted is discussed in part D.) But to say that an exemption is permitted, the Court concluded, "is not to say that it is constitutionally required, and that the appropriate occasions for its creation can be discerned by the courts."

Thus *Smith* adopts the position of Justice Harlan in *Sherbert*: accommodations are permitted but not required. *Smith* does not require facially equal treatment for religious and other conduct; it merely says that equal treatment satisfies the Constitution, and that the political branches may decide whether to protect religion distinctively. Smith's rule thus shows influences of the principle of equal treatment between religion and non-religion, but also of a posture of deference to the government.

The chief issue after *Smith* be will be to determine when a law is "neutral and generally applicable." Will the courts look behind a facially neutral law and find that the state intended to restrict religion in particular? And how many exemptions for other activities will it take to show that a law is not generally applicable? The *Lukumi* decision protecting Santeria animal sacrifices (see part A–2 above), decided after *Smith*, suggests that the Court will look behind a law's face. The ordinances there were also ruled not generally applicable, but they contained so many exemptions for various kinds of animal killing that the Court viewed the case as easy. It is still uncertain if very many other free exercise claims will be recognized under the *Smith* test.

One interesting example of a post-*Smith* issue concerning a law's "general applicability" is the question whether the trustee of the estate of a bankrupt debtor may recover contributions made by the debtor to her church during a one-year period before the bankruptcy filing. The Bankruptcy Code, in section 548, authorizes such recovery of any transfer for which the debtor has not received "reasonably equivalent value." When trustees have sought to use this provision to recover the debtors' tithes in order to benefit creditors, churches have argued that such an application would be unconstitutional because the provision authorizing recovery is not "generally applicable" but is full of exceptions. The trustee is not empowered to reach transactions where the debtor paid money for consumption goods (such as food or even gambling), and in addition many durable goods bought during the one-year period before filing would be exempt from creditors under other parts of the Code. But trustees argue that these other transactions are different because the Code seeks not just to maximize creditors' recovery, but also to protect third parties (if they have paid "equivalent value") and to ensure the debtor a "fresh start" (hence the exemptions for various durable goods). (The bankruptcy issue also raises the question of whether maximizing the recovery of creditors is a "compelling" governmental interest. See, e.g., *In re Young* (8th Cir.1996).

C. OTHER BASES FOR PROTECTION OF RELIGIOUS CONDUCT AGAINST GENERAL LAWS

As just noted above, the exceptions to *Smith*'s rule—cases of hybrid rights and individualized assessments—could, if read broadly, continue to give protection to religious conduct from laws that are generally applicable. In addition, there are other bases on which religious believers and groups might assert such protection.

1. The Religion Clauses: Institutional Autonomy and Non–Entanglement

a. The "Internal Autonomy" Decisions

Notwithstanding the government's power to regulate religious conduct generally, a brief passage in *Smith* states that government still may not "lend its power to one or the other side in controversies over religious dogma." *Id.* This language, together with the citations following it, suggests that the Court continues to believe that religious institutions have rights of "internal" autonomy that have been recognized in previous decisions. Those rulings prevent the government from interfering in certain ways in matters or disputes that are internal to the religious organization. The institutional autonomy decisions typically involve intra-church disputes about who will lead the organization or control its property. Two rules have emerged.

In a number of decisions the Court has held that government, including civil courts, may not interfere in internal disputes and must defer to the resolution of the dispute by the highest authority within the church. This approach crystallized long ago in *Watson v. Jones* (S.Ct.1872), which arose when a Kentucky Presbyterian congregation split over the national denomination's condemnation of former slaveholders and Confederate rebels, and then both sides in the dispute claimed title to the church property. The Supreme Court ruled for the national side, basing its decision not on the First Amendment (which had not yet been applied to state actions), but on general principles of federal common law; these principles, however, have continued to be followed under the Religion Clauses.

Watson held that the right of religious freedom includes the right to organize religious bodies and "to establish tribunals for the decision of questions arising among" the members. By joining the organization voluntarily, all members give "implied consent to this government, and are bound to submit to it." (This principle was converted into a First Amendment holding in *Kedroff v. St. Nicholas Cathedral* (S.Ct.1952), which stated that the Free Exercise Clause guarantees religious organizations "power to decide for themselves, free from state interference, matters of church government as well as those of faith and doctrine.")

Watson then concluded that the national Presbyterian denomination was a hierarchically organized church, in which the decision of the highest tribunal was binding. A secular court could not review that decision or second-guess the tribunal's interpretation of the church's own rules and customs. This same principle, deference to the rulings of the highest church tribunal, has been applied to a number of other American denominations as well. In *Kedroff, supra,* the Court applied the principle to strike down a New York statute that attempted to transfer control over Russian Orthodox church property and affairs in the United States away from the mother church in Moscow and over to a new American organization free from the influence of the Soviet Union. The Orthodox church was plainly hierarchical in form, and the ecclesiastical leaders in Moscow had never authorized the transfer of control.

But under the *Watson* approach, if a local church was part of a body organized on "independent" lines—where ultimate authority rested in the individual congregations, who merely affiliated together—then the secular court's resolution of any disputes was different. The court would follow the ordinary legal principles governing voluntary associations, which usually would give the disputed property to the local congregation. Thus the *Watson* approach called for the court to determine what sort of "polity" the religious body followed—hierarchical or congregational—and defer to either the hierarchy or the congregation, according to which was the ultimate locus of authority.

The *Watson* "polity" approach, however, received strong criticism on the ground that it produced too much deference to church authority by civil courts. Even if a church is hierarchical in its overall structure, control over some particular issue (for example, a certain piece of property), might be given by the parties to some lower body (such as the local congregation) through a deed, conveyance, or other instrument. In such a case, critics argue, deference to the hierarchy would upset the arrangements made within the community and would violate the free exercise rights of the local body. Moreover, the Court itself later warned, in some religious bodies "the locus of control would be ambiguous" and a court would have to make theological decisions based on "a searching and therefore impermissible inquiry into church polity" (*Jones v. Wolf* (1979)).

Based on these misgivings about the polity approach, the Court in *Jones v. Wolf* approved a second means of resolving disputes over church property: the application of "neutral principles" of trust or property law that are used in comparable litigation between secular parties. To decide which faction owns contested property, courts may look at "the language of the deeds, the terms of the local church charters, the state statutes governing the holding of church property, and the provisions in the constitution of the general church concerning the ownership and control of church property."

Reading secular and church documents in the light of neutral principles of law may produce quite a different result from how the church tribunals would rule. For example, one state court allowed a parish that broke away from a Russian Orthodox denomination—unquestionably a hierarchical body—to take the church building and land because of the language in the property deeds and the parish by-laws. *Primate and Bishops' Synod v. Church of the Holy Resurrection* (Mass.1994).

Under *Jones v. Wolf*, states are generally free to apply neutral principles of law to internal disputes, although they may also choose to defer to the church's own internal tribunals. *Jones* thus parallels the general free exercise rule of *Employment Division v. Smith* that the government does not have to exempt religious conduct from neutral and generally applicable laws although it may do so.

However, in some cases the Court still insists on abstention by civil courts and deference to the church's internal decisions. One situation, according to *Jones* itself, is when looking to neutral principles of law still requires the court to interpret religious concepts such as those often found in a church constitution; if such interpretation is required, the court must defer to the resolution by the church's own body. Second, in cases where the dispute involves not just control over church property, but control over the direction of the church itself, the Court indicated that deference is appropriate rather than the application of neutral principles.

Both of these factors were present in *Serbian Orthodox Diocese v. Milivojevich* (S.Ct.1976). There the mother church had removed an American bishop from his position, but an Illinois state court overturned the removal on the ground that the proceedings had failed to follow the church's own rules. The Supreme Court reversed and let the defrocking go forward, on the ground that the state court's ruling had impermissibly (i) passed on theological and not just secular questions and (ii) resolved not just a property dispute but a dispute over who would exercise pastoral authority in the church.

Another example of the principle that civil courts may not interpret religious concepts is the holding that courts may not award disputed church property to a claimant on the basis that the opposing claimant has departed from church doctrine. *Presbyterian Church v. Hull Church* (S.Ct.1969). In that case, local churches withdrew from a Presbyterian denomination and claimed the church property, even though it was held in trust for the denomination, on the ground that the denomination had departed from fundamental theological doctrines. Although this "departure from doctrine" principle had long roots in English trust law, the Court held it unconstitutional on the ground that it "would require the civil courts to engage in the forbidden process of interpreting and weighing church doctrine."

In summary, the internal autonomy decisions after *Jones v. Wolf* indicate that a state may apply neutral, secular rules of law to many internal disputes—especially to those simply over property. But when the application of legal rules involves the interpretation of religious concepts, or a controversy over who will lead the church, it appears that courts still should defer to the decision of the church's own highest authority. In such cases, a religious organization can still assert a right to autonomy even in the face of a general state law.

b. Non–Entanglement Under the Establishment Clause

Another potential means for religious organizations to challenge general laws that intrude on their autonomy was, ironically, first set forth in decisions that struck down government aid to religious institutions as an establishment of religion (see Chapter 5). *Lemon v. Kurtzman* (S.Ct.1971) invalidated a law giving salary supplements to parochial school teachers even though the law forbade the subsidized teachers to teach religion in their classes. The Court found this restriction itself unconstitutional because enforcing it would require a "comprehensive" and "continuing" surveillance of the teachers' activities. The result would be an "excessive entanglement of church and state"—historically a concern of the Establishment Clause because established churches had not only received government support but had also been subject to government oversight. This so-called non-entanglement prong was often used by the Court to strike down government aid programs because of the regulation that accompanied the aid.

Could the non-entanglement principle be used not only to bar aid that comes with regulation, but to bar regulation in the first place? Such a use seems appropriate, since the non-entanglement principle was based in the first place on the religious school's interest in freedom from government surveillance.

One Supreme Court decision has suggested that religious entities could use the Establishment Clause as a significant shield against regulation. The Court refused to allow the National Labor Relations Board to assert jurisdiction over teachers in church-operated elementary and secondary schools, on the ground that such regulation—that is, regulation of unionization and collective bargaining—would create "a significant risk" of entanglement between church and state. *NLRB v. Catholic Bishop of Chicago* (S.Ct.1979).

Citing the decisions barring government aid to teachers, the Court noted "the critical and unique role of the teacher in fulfilling the mission of the church-operated school" and pointed out that the Board's mandate to oversee "terms and conditions of employment" of teachers would allow it to intervene in "nearly everything that goes on in the schools." The Court did not actually find that regulation would violate the First Amendment; instead, it held that the "significant risk" of unconstitutional entanglement meant that Congress should express an "affirmative intention" to give the Board jurisdiction over parochial school teachers, and no such affirmative intention was present.

However, *Catholic Bishop* has not generated other decisions shielding religious institutions from government regulation. This may be because the decision was technically only an interpretation of the labor statute, or perhaps because courts conclude that other regulations involve less pervasive oversight of an institution's activities than the collective bargaining laws do. Thus, recent decisions have held that the application to religious institutions of federal minimum-wage laws and of state sales taxes do not create excessive entanglement. *Tony and Susan Alamo Foundation v. Secretary of Labor* (S.Ct.1985) (minimum wage); *Jimmy Swaggart, supra* (sales tax). Both regimes imposed only "administrative and recordkeeping requirements" and thus were not unacceptably "intrusive into religious affairs." *Id.* Arguments based on non-entanglement have also often failed in lower courts.

2. Federal Legislation: The Religious Freedom Restoration Act and Its (Partial?) Invalidation

The decision in *Smith* angered religious and civil liberties groups, who turned to the alternative of federal legislation: they pressed Congress to enact a statute reinstating the compelling interest test. The unusually broad coalition included conservatives such as the Traditional Values Coalition and liberals such as People for the American Way. In response, Congress overwhelmingly passed the Religious Freedom Restoration of Act of 1993. RFRA provided that government may not "substantially burden" a person's exercise of religion, even by a rule of general applicability, unless it can show that the burden furthers a "compelling governmental interest" and is "the least restrictive means" of furthering it. The statute thus purported "to restore the compelling interest test as set forth in *Sherbert* [and] *Yoder*."

However, the Supreme Court recently invalidated RFRA, at least as applied to state and local government actions, in *City of Boerne v. Flores* (S.Ct.1997) (see part B–2 above). In applying RFRA to states, Congress—which of course can only act in reliance on some constitutionally enumerated power—had invoked section 5 of the Fourteenth Amendment, which gives it power to "enforce the provisions" of the Amendment "by appropriate legislation." RFRA was designed to enforce the free exercise right, which is indeed included in the Fourteenth Amendment through the incorporation of the First Amendment. *Boerne*, however, held that the RFRA exceeded the section 5 power because it did not appropriately "enforce" the constitutional free exercise rule—that is, the rule of *Smith*—but rather rejected *Smith* and "attempt[ed] a substantive change in constitutional protections." To allow Congress to declare such changes under section 5, the justices said, would remove any restrictions on its legislative power, upsetting the federal-state balance.

Before *Boerne*, there had been debate whether section 5 empowered Congress simply to develop specific remedies for constitutional violations that the Court would recognize, or to go further and base legislation on its own substantive constitutional interpretation. *Boerne* squarely held that Congress's power was remedial only and not substantive, hearkening back to the statement of *Marbury v. Madison* (S.Ct.1803) statement that it is the province of the courts to say what the law is.

The Court concluded that RFRA could not be read as a remedial statute enforcing the nondiscrimination rule of *Smith*, because it was far "out of proportion" to such a goal. The Act applied to any substantial burden imposed on religion, but the Court noted that many laws impose such burdens without aiming at or discriminating against religion. Once the Act's stringent compelling interest test applied, "laws valid under *Smith* would fall without regard to whether they had the object or purpose of stifling free exercise."

The Court distinguished RFRA from provisions of the federal Voting Rights Act of 1965, which also bars certain state actions affecting the right to vote even though the underlying provision, the Fifteenth Amendment, prohibits only intentional denials of the vote. These restrictions, the Court said, were narrower in scope than RFRA or terminated after a certain period, and were aimed at particular acts or states that had a history of intentionally denying the vote. However, despite the Court's distinctions, the invalidation of RFRA still called into question other provisions of the Voting Rights Act (especially the extremely important section 2), as well as other civil rights laws covering state and local governments.

One chief question now is whether RFRA remains valid insofar as it restricts federal government actions. The *Boerne* ruling interpreted the scope of section 5 of the Fourteenth Amendment. Congress's power to limit various federal government actions is based not on the Fourteenth Amendment (which limits only states and their subdivisions), but presumably on the various enumerated powers in Article I together with the power to make laws "necessary and proper" for executing the other powers (Art. I, § 8, cl. 18). Thus, under its power to raise armies, Congress may deem it necessary and proper to exempt conscientious objectors from military service. *Welsh v. United States* (S.Ct.1970) (White, J., dissenting on other grounds); *EEOC v. Catholic University* (D.C. Cir.1996) (holding that Congress could, through RFRA, amend Title VII to protect religious institutions from liability for discrimination). RFRA simply supplants or reinforces those specific exemptions with a general one running through all federal law, a course that (it is asserted) Congress could likewise deem necessary and proper. When Congress applied RFRA to federal laws, one can argue, it did not impose its judgment on anyone else (as with the application to state laws), but merely restrained itself from burdening religious exercise through the laws it enacts. See *Boerne* (stating that "within its sphere of power and responsibilities," Congress may "make its own informed judgment on the meaning and force of the Constitution").

However, some critics have asserted that RFRA is unconstitutional even as applied to federal laws because it violates the seperation of powers—that by explicitly rejecting the rule of *Smith* and legislating a different across-the-board rule for religious claims, Congress in effect tried to amend the Free Exercise Clause and interfered with the judicial power to interpret the Constitution (*Marbury*). This argument might find some support in a few references to separation of powers in *Boerne*, but the argument also faces difficulties. As the critics concede, Congress can sometimes legislate to protect religious exercise even where the Court would not find a constitutional right (see part D). The critics' complaint therefore must be with the fact that RFRA's protection is general and across the board: but Congress may have had legitimate reasons for choosing to create a general statutory standard, for example to ensure that all religious claims are given equal consideration.

Attention in Congress after *Boerne* shifted to finding other possible grounds of power to protect religious conduct where *Smith* would not. To support a general, wide-ranging statute like RFRA, Congress might rely on its Article I power to "tax and spend for the general welfare" and require that all state programs or agencies receiving federal funds refrain from burdening religious exercise. It might even rely on its power to regulate interstate commerce and protect those religious practices that affect interstate commerce—for example, the building of a church or the employment of church workers—although this might be seen as an overly broad assertion of the Commerce Power. Or Congress might legislate to enforce the Free Exercise Clause as interpreted in *Smith*, perhaps by (i) shifting the burden to the government to prove nondiscrimination; (ii) protecting religion in the "hybrid rights" and "individualized assessments" situations mentioned by *Smith*; or (iii) making specific findings that in certain areas (such as zoning or historic preservation disputes), even facially neutral laws tend to single out religion for discriminatory burdens.

3. State Constitutional Protection of Religious Conduct

Advocates of religious accommodations after *Smith* also turned to state constitutions and their religious freedom provisions. States, of course, are free to give greater scope to religious exercise or other constitutional rights than the federal Constitution gives. (The only caveat is that the state must not take its accommodation of religion so far that it establishes religion; see part D.) Some states have followed the equal treatment rule of *Smith* in interpreting their own religion provisions. See, e.g., *Elsaesser v. City of Hamilton Board of Zoning Appeals* (Ohio App.1990). But other states have made clear, both before and after *Smith*, that their religious freedom provisions are independent of and more protective than the federal provision. See, e.g., *State v. Hershberger* (Minn.1990) (religious freedom); *Kentucky State Board for Education v. Rudasill* (Ky.1979) (religious upbringing of children).

There are two common reasons why some state constitutional provisions are interpreted more broadly than the Free Exercise Clause. Both are displayed in a Washington Supreme Court decision holding that a generally applicable historic preservation ordinance could not apply to churches. *First*

Covenant Church v. City of Seattle (Wash.1992). First, the text of the state provision may be more specific or demanding. For example, the Washington provision gives "absolute freedom of conscience" except for "practices inconsistent with the peace and safety of the state." The Washington court found this language more demanding than the federal ban (on laws "prohibiting" free exercise), and ruled that it protected religious exercise even against general laws.

The more specific and demanding language led the Washington majority to apply the compelling interest standard, a course that several other state courts have taken. (The court ruled that preserving architecture was not a compelling purpose.) But a concurring justice took a somewhat different approach, one that other courts have also used. According to the concurrence, the "peace and safety" language, which is common in state constitutions, explicitly limits the kinds of interests that can justify restrictions on religious freedom. However compelling the goal of architectural preservation is, it does not protect peace or safety and therefore, according to the concurrence, could not be applied to restrict the church's activity.

In addition to interpreting a different text, a state court may simply believe that *Smith*'s conception of religious liberty is too limited. For example, the Washington court in *First Covenant Church* argued that *Smith*'s "rule places minority religions at a disadvantage. Our court, conversely, has rejected the idea that a political majority may control a minority's right of free exercise through the political process."

D. LEGISLATIVE ACCOMMODATIONS OF RELIGION: THE SCOPE OF PERMITTED ACCOMMODATIONS UNDER THE ESTABLISHMENT CLAUSE

So far, this chapter has discussed broad rules requiring accommodations under the federal Constitution, federal statutes, or state constitutions. But religious practice is often exempted from a law by action of the legislature that passed the law or the administrative agency that enforces it. Such accommodations by the political branches are common; the statute books are full of them.

Litigants have sometimes challenged legislative accommodations as violating the Establishment Clause. Thus, this subject returns us to the discussion above (part B–2) on whether exemptions for religion constitute impermissible government favoritism. This discussion applies not only to legislative exemptions, but to constitutional exemptions; if exemptions are impermissible favoritism for religion, then a fortiori they should not be required by the Constitution either. But some critics have argued that accommodations by the political branches are especially suspect because they are likely to reflect the power of majority or politically-active faiths.

1. A Brief Sampling of Legislative Accommodations of Religious Institutions or Activities

There are hundreds, even thousands, of provisions in federal and state statutes and regulations that accommodate religious practices, wholly or partially, to take account of the effect that a certain law will have on such practices. What follows are just a few examples.

Some of these accommodations or exemptions include religious practices simply as part of a broader exemption available to other groups. Religious organizations are exempt from federal income taxes and (usually) state property taxes, and contributions to such organizations are deductible from the contributions' income taxes—but the same is true for a wide range of other educational, civic, and charitable organizations. See *Walz v. Tax Commission* (S.Ct.1970) (noting that property tax exemptions extend also to "hospitals, libraries, playgrounds, [and] scientific, professional, historical and patriotic groups").

Other accommodations or exemptions are extended more specifically to religious organizations. The federal statute prohibiting religious discrimination in employment, Title VII of the Civil Rights Act of 1964, allows religion-based hiring by "religious organizations" and by colleges or universities that are substantially "owned, supported, controlled, or managed by" a religious body. Religious organizations may also prefer members of their own faith in certain kinds of housing, under provisions of the

Fair Housing Act. There are partial exemptions from federal laws against gambling and against making copies of copyrighted works, when those activities are engaged in by religious organizations. At the state and local level, some states exempt religiously affiliated schools, or religiously based home schooling, from certain kinds of state educational regulations. Some local ordinances preserving architectural landmarks exempt churches, or at last allow churches to make certain changes in their buildings.

Other legislative exemptions from general laws protect the religious beliefs or activity of individuals. The federal draft laws exempt ministers and those who object to military service on religious grounds. Federal drug laws, as well as those in a number of states, exempt the use of peyote in religious ceremonies (even though the Supreme Court in *Smith* held that no exemption was constitutionally required). In various states, parents may object on religious grounds to having their children immunized, or to sending their children to school after a certain age; and prayers or other forms of religiously healing practices are excepted from laws prohibiting child endangerment or requiring that parents seek medical care.

2. Decisions and Arguments Upholding Legislative Accommodations

We first discuss decisions in which the Court has upheld provisions that exempt religious practices from legal restrictions. It is important to note at the outset that the Court has readily upheld such exemptions when religious activity is exempted as part of a broader exemption extended to other activities as well. Such was the case with the property tax exemptions upheld in *Walz, supra*, which the Court noted included church property "within a broad class of property owned by nonprofit, quasi-public corporations." Such exemptions are easily upheld because they serve both religious liberty and equality, exempting religious activity from regulation but on the same terms as many other activities.

The question has been more difficult, however, when the legislative exemption extends only to religious organizations or activity (for the same reasons that it was more difficult to decide whether such exemptions are ever constitutionally required; see part B). Indeed, a plurality of the Court later stated that the tax exemption in *Walz* had been upheld against Establishment Clause challenge only because it extended to many other organizations as well: "[t]he breadth of [the] property tax exemption was essential to our holding," a plurality said in *Texas Monthly v. Bullock* (S.Ct.1989) (striking down a tax exemption that extended only to religious organizations). As we will see, the Court's decisions have been much more mixed with respect to full-fledged "accommodations"—where the legislature exempts religious activity from a law generally applicable to others.

Nevertheless, the law seems clear that some accommodations for religion are permissible. As already noted, the *Smith* decision, even as it rejected the compelled exemptions doctrine, suggested that the political branches were permitted to enact "nondiscriminatory religious-practice exemptions." Several other decisions have upheld particular accommodations against Establishment Clause challenges. *Zorach v. Clauson* (S.Ct.1952), for example, upheld a program releasing public school students to attend religious education classes off school premises (see Chapter 4). The Court said that when the state "accommodates the public schedule to [citizens'] spiritual needs," it "follows the best of our traditions"; and to forbid such actions would show "a callous indifference to religious groups." *Zorach* remains good law in favor of legislative accommodations, although some of its broad language (such as "We are a religious people whose institutions presuppose a Supreme Being") might not command a majority of the Court today. See also *Trans World Airlines v. Hardison* (S.Ct.1977) (upholding Title VII provision that requires employers to make "reasonable accommodations" to employees' religious needs, although construing the employer's duty narrowly); *Gillette v. United States*, *supra* (approving draft exemption for those with religious conscientious objections to all wars).

The Court also upheld a Title VII provision that exempts religious organizations from the rule against discriminating in employment on the basis of religion. *Corporation of Presiding Bishop v. Amos* (S.Ct.1987). The exemption had originally shielded religious employment preferences only in the organization's "religious" activities, but it was later extended to all activities. A janitor at a gymnasium owned by the Mormon Church failed to continue to meet the Church's religious requirements for the job, was fired, and sued. The Court assumed that the broader exemption for all of a religious organization's activities was not required by the Free Exercise Clause but nevertheless upheld it against Establishment Clause challenge. Applying the *Lemon v. Kurtzman* test (see Chapter 1), the Court found that the exemption had the permissible purpose and effect of relieving a "significant burden" on religious activity, including the burden of predicting, "on pain of substantial liability, . . . which of its activities a secular court will consider religious."

Reading the "secular effect" prong of *Lemon* in light of a concern for the organization's religious liberty, the Court held that "[a] law is not unconstitutional simply because it **allows** churches to advance religion"; the *Lemon* test is violated only when "the **government itself** has advanced religion through its own activities and influence." *Id.* (emphasis in original). This distinction between government's advancing religion itself and government's freeing private individuals and groups to advance religion constitutes the theoretical basis for accommodations of religious practice.

Despite the Court's broad language, some commentators have argued that *Amos* is a narrow decision that does not validate a wide range of accommodations. First, although the Title VII exemption was unanimously upheld, a majority of the justices stated in concurring opinions that the holding extended only to non-profit activities of religious organizations (such as the gymnasium in question), as opposed to for-profit activities. Justice Brennan, for example, argued that even as the exemption promoted the organization's autonomy, it also burdened the religious liberty of employees by exposing them to employers' religious discrimination. Balancing these concerns led to the conclusion that the exemption was permissible for non-profit activities (which are likely to be significantly religious), but possibly not so for profit-making activities (where secular concerns would likely predominate and thus the religious interest was not strong enough to justify special treatment).

Brennan and the other justices did not see accommodation as having the sole effect of unburdening religious practice. They also started from another baseline, assuming regulation of all entities, and considered whether exemption of religious entities could also have some effect of helping them to burden individuals' religious liberty.

Second, the matter of religious discrimination by religious organizations could be seen as a particularly compelling case for accommodation. The rule against religious discrimination in employment affects religious entities disproportionately; they alone have an ideological interest in having their activities conducted by persons of the same religious faith. By way of comparison, the Sierra Club is free to require that all its employees show a commitment to environmental goals; no law forbids employers to discriminate on the basis of ideology. Thus, a law forbidding religious organizations to engage in religious preferences could be seen as itself discriminatory: denying them the freedom, enjoyed by other ideological organizations, to ensure that their employees support their ideological goals. Indeed, a rule against religious discrimination in employment, while perhaps generally applicable under *Smith*, may not be "neutral" as to religion, since it specifically mentions the term.

3. Decisions and Arguments Limiting Legislative Accommodations

However broad the approval of legislative accommodations was in *Zorach* and *Amos*, in some other decisions the Court has taken a circumscribed view of accommodations and has struck down certain ones.

a. Accommodations for a Single Sect

The simplest rule involves accommodations extended only to a particular faith when other, similarly situated believers are not exempted. Such discrimination between sects is clearly prohibited by the Establishment Clause (see *Larson v. Valente*, (S.Ct.1982), cited in Chapter 1) (striking down ordinance that regulated only those religious organizations that solicit more than 50 percent of their funds from non-members)). Discriminatory treatment violates the agreed-upon principle of equality between religions, and also could not be justified as promoting religious liberty or choice for all.

The Supreme Court applied this principle to strike down an accommodation in *Board of Education, Kiryas Joel School District v. Grumet* (S.Ct. 1994) (see also Chapter 4). There the New York legislature carved out a public school district to correspond to the boundaries of a village of Orthodox Hasidic Jews, the Satmarer, who follow insular and traditionalist customs concerning family life, dress, and manner of appearance. The district was designed to permit disabled children in the sect to receive special education services (to which state and federal law entitled them) without their having to travel to nearby public schools, where they had been "traumatized" by the very different manners and customs of the majority of children. (At the time, Establishment Clause case law forbade the state to provide the classes in the village's religious schools. See *Grand Rapids v. Ball* and *Aguilar v. Felton*, discussed in Chapter 5.) But in a lawsuit brought by state taxpayers, the Supreme Court invalidated the statute creating the district.

The majority held that the creation of the district failed the test of neutrality toward religion because it could not be certain that "the benefit received by the Satmar community is one that the legislature will provide equally to other religious (and nonreligious) groups." In dissent, Justice Scalia argued that the principle of equality between groups did not forbid the district because the Hasidim were the only group that apparently had any expressed need for a separate district because of their conscientiously motivated practices. He argued that the

Court should not pronounce discrimination until the legislature refused to act on a similar claim by another group in the future. But the majority responded that such a failure to act by the legislature could not be easily reviewed, so the only safe course was to strike down the district at the outset.

Some of the majority's language suggested that the Court believed that any group seeking a special district to accommodate its conscientious practice must receive one, whether or not it was religious: that is, that at least in this context, the Establishment Clause would forbid accommodating religious needs while not accommodating secular ones. But elsewhere the majority pulled back from this holding, which would cast doubt on all religious exemptions. It reiterated the approval of religious accommodations in *Zorach* and *Amos,* and distinguished those decisions on the ground that the Kiryas Joel accommodation was limited to a single sect (citing *Larson, supra*). Thus the holding of *Kiryas Joel* (as opposed to the broader dicta) seems to be only that government may not enact a law that explicitly accommodates only a single religious sect.

However, in other decisions the Court has struck down legislative accommodations that extended to all religions affected in a particular context. *Estate of Thornton v. Caldor, Inc.* (S.Ct.1985) invalidated a statute giving any employee in the state the right to refuse to work on his Sabbath. And *Texas Monthly v. Bullock* (S.Ct.1989) struck down a provision of state sales tax laws exempting the sales of books and periodicals whose contents were solely religious. These decisions advanced various arguments that would have varying consequences for legislative exemptions as a whole.

b. *Burdens Removed from Religion, Versus Burdens Imposed on Others*

First, both decisions evince a concern that religious exemptions not go so far as to create incentives for religious belief or impose significant burdens on nonbelievers. For example, in *Thornton* the Court found that the statute reflected an "unyielding weighting of Sabbath observers over all other interests": there were no adjustments to protect other employees who would have to fill in for Sabbath observers, or those employers who would suffer "substantial economic burdens" from the unavailability of workers. Thus the statute went beyond accommodating religious practice to "impermissibly advanc[ing]" it.

Similarly, in *Texas Monthly* the plurality opinion (written by Justice Brennan) set forth an analysis asking whether the exemption (a) removed "a significant state-imposed deterrent to the free exercise of religion" and (b) "burden[ed] non-beneficiaries markedly." The sales tax exemption failed because sales taxes did not seriously burden religious publications (no one had claimed that paying the taxes violated his religious tenets), and because the exemption burdened other publications and citizens who would probably have to make up for tax revenue lost by the exemption. In a footnote, the plurality opinion approved of *Zorach* and *Amos*—two decisions that had upheld religious accommodations—but distinguished them on the ground that they removed more serious burdens to religion or did not impose serious burdens on others.

Although such an analysis—weighing the burdens removed from religion with those imposed on others—has been prominent in the decisions, it has never been fully adopted by the Court majority. But it does offer advantages. It permits the Court to explain why it has approved some legislative accommodations but struck down others. The analysis can also be defended as consistent with an overall "religious choice" approach: government may exempt religious exercise from a general law that imposes serious burdens on the choice to practice religion, but not when the exemption in turn imposes disproportionate costs on others who have chosen not to practice religion. However, critics of legislative accommodations have argued (as Justice Scalia did concerning compelled accommodations in *Smith*) that there is no way to perform such a "balancing" between the interests of religious believers and of other citizens: it is like comparing apples and oranges. Such a balancing approach, the critics maintain, will always produce inconsistent and unconvincing results.

c. *Other Arguments Against Legislative Accommodations*

Two other arguments that appeared in *Thornton* and *Texas Monthly* (although not in majority opinions) might place broader restrictions on any legislative accommodation of religion that does not extend to non-religious conduct as well. Justice Brennan's *Texas Monthly* opinion objected that the tax exemption for religious publications did not extend to non-religious publications that could also be seen as addressing the same issues as religious publications do. The opinion distinguished *Walz v. Tax Commission* (S.Ct.1970), which had upheld property tax exemptions for religious organizations, on the ground that the exemption there simply included religious organizations among a wide range of non-profit community groups.

If this rationale were broadly followed, then many religious exemptions might be impermissible because corresponding non-religious groups would have to .be exempted as well. In other words, the Establishment Clause would forbid any unequal accommodation for religion. However, the argument was immediately qualified: Brennan's opinion acknowledged that the Free Exercise Clause might require special protection for religious activity, although it concluded that no significant free exercise interest was involved.

For several reasons, *Texas Monthly* could be read narrowly so as not to forbid a great many legislative accommodations. First, the case involved a a tax exemption, which Justice Brennan's plurality opinion compared to a financial subsidy. Perhaps the opinion means only that when government confers an explicitly financial benefit, it must do so without favoring religion. As noted above, the financial benefits of tax exemptions may attract people in a way that exemptions for other religious conduct—such as refusing medical treatment—would not.

Moreover, *Texas Monthly* involved publications and speech. It may be that the requirement of equal treatment between religion and non-religion is particularly strong in that context, since the Free Speech and Free Press clauses of the First Amendment protect expression in general and not merely religious expression. Indeed, Justice White concurred in striking down the exemption in *Texas Monthly*, but under the Free Press Clause rather than the Establishment Clause. One might argue that religious conduct can receive distinctive protection because of the Free Exercise Clause, but that religious activity in the form of speech must be treated the same as other expression because of the requirement of "content neutrality" in free speech law (see, e.g., part A–2).

Another broad concern with legislative exemptions appeared in a concurring opinion in *Thornton*: Justice O'Connor objected that the Sabbath observance statute protected only one form of religious practice, thus communicating a message of favoritism for those particular beliefs. This argument recalls the contention, noted above, that legislative accommodations in particular statutes are especially suspect because each protects only a particular form of religious practice, which may have gained protection because of its political power. The logical conclusion of this theory is that the only permissible legislative exemptions would be those, such as the

Religious Freedom Restoration Act, that are so broad as to cover all religious practices.

However, no Court majority has ever adopted this argument against accommodations or exemptions. It should be pointed out that a legislature may enact an exemption to a specific law not because the legislature favors the particular religion affected, but because this specific conflict has come to its attention and needs to be addressed. Justice O'Connor's concurrence in *Thornton* expressed approval of the Title VII provision that generally requires reasonable accommodation of employees' religious practices—even though only certain religious practices, and not all, are likely to conflict with workplace rules.

Overall, then, the Court has several times struck down legislative accommodations, but it has always been careful to reaffirm that some such accommodations are constitutional. *Texas Monthly*, as we have noted, distinguished *Amos* and *Zorach* as removing more substantial burdens on religion. And *Kiryas Joel* cited all the cases that have upheld accommodations before striking down the Satmar school district on the ground that it was sect-specific.

Thus, the decisions on the permissibility of religious accommodations can be seen as reflecting an uneasy tension between the values of (a) equal treatment and (b) religious liberty or choice. An unbending insistence on equal treatment between religion and other activities would forbid all religious accommodations. The only way the government could protect religious liberty from regulation would be to repeal the regulation for all citizens affected—or at least for all citizens who have some conscientious or ideologically-based objection to the law. The Court has not required this. It has sometimes distinguished between permissible and impermissible exemptions on the ground that the exemption would impose greater burdens on others than it removed from religious believers; this analysis suggest a focus on the value of religious choice, and whether an exemption for religion alone distorts such choice. But the Court has found a number of accommodations unconstitutional, reflecting the continuing importance of the value of equal treatment.

Conclusion

To sum up the discussion of the current law of free exercise: The government must generally treat religious expression and conduct no worse than it treats other forms of speech or conduct. Moreover, under the federal Constitution, the political branches have some discretion to exempt religious conduct from the burdens of even a general law, thereby departing from equal treatment, in order to respect religious liberty and choice. However, that discretion is limited by the Establishment Clause, although the exact limits are not clear from the Court's decisions. And the government is almost never constitutionally required to make such accommodations; under *Employment Division v.*

Smith, treating religious and non-religious conduct the same under a generally applicable law almost always satisfies the Free Exercise Clause. Accommodations for religion may be required at the state level, however, under state constitutional provisions.

CHAPTER FOUR
RELIGION IN GOVERNMENT INSTITUTIONS AND ACTIVITIES

Overview

Having discussed issues concerning the free exercise of religion, we now turn to contexts in which the other religion provision, the Establishment Clause, has been important. One especially controversial subject has been the presence of religious elements in government institutions and activities—most notably in the public schools but also in other governmental facilities, programs, and statements, from courthouse Christmas displays to invocations at presidential inaugurations.

The Court has often held that the Establishment Clause forbids government from conducting religious exercises, such as prayers or scriptural readings, or endorsing or favoring any religious doctrine. It has applied these principles especially strictly in the public schools, on the ground that children are especially vulnerable to pressures, even subtle ones, from the government. Private religious activity in schools has been protected in a series of decisions, but religious activity by the school itself is forbidden. Government religious activities have been struck down even when objecting students were theoretically free to leave: the Court has often insisted that government must not merely refrain from coercing anyone to practice religion, but must be "neutral" altogether toward religion.

Outside the schools, however, the record is more mixed; the Court has upheld prayers in state legislatures and some kinds of government-sponsored religious symbols, although it has struck down others. The seeming inconsistencies in these decisions have prompted criticisms both from commentators and from some justices.

The sometimes jumbled mosaic of decisions stems from several different underlying concerns. The rule against government-sponsored religious activities reflects both a concern for the status of those who do not adhere to the favored faith, and a concern that even the favored faith will be corrupted by government influence. But this principle has also had to be reconciled with two other notions, both of which reflect the fact that government is a pervasive presence in the culture.

First, while the Establishment Clause forbids government-sponsored religion, the Free Exercise and Free Speech clauses protect religious speech and activity by private individuals and groups. Such activity often occurs in governmental settings such as public schools, and so courts have had to draw the line between government-sponsored and citizen-initiated religion.

Second, religion has been historically, and still is today, an important part of culture, and if government seeks to reflect American culture it must acknowledge the role of religion. Throughout history, American governments have made religious proclamations, statements, and references, usually of a generic Christian or monotheistic variety. If government must be neutral toward religion, are some or all of these common practices unconstitutional? If so, is the real role of religion in American history and culture being artificially ignored—thus making the government hostile to religion rather than neutral? Or can lines be drawn between acknowledging religion and promoting it? The varying decisions reflect the Court's struggles with these questions.

A. RELIGIOUS ELEMENTS IN THE PUBLIC SCHOOLS

The issues in this chapter can be examined by looking at the Court's numerous decisions concerning religious elements in the public schools. The Court has shown a "heightened concern with protecting freedom of conscience from subtle coercive pressures in the elementary and secondary schools." *Lee v. Weisman* (S.Ct.1992).

Behind this concern lies the fact that children are especially susceptible to pressure from authority figures such as teachers and principals—as well as the notion that in public schools matters that deeply divide Americans, such as religious doctrines, should be put aside so that children can be instructed in a set of common values for good citizenship. This attitude found its strongest expression in Justice Frankfurter's statement that public schools are "a symbol of our secular unity" and therefore "must keep scrupulously free from entanglement in the strife of sects." *McCollum v. Board of Education* (S.Ct.1948) (Frankfurter, J., concurring). But if the sensitive nature of educating children leads many people to oppose religious teaching in public schools, it leads many others to oppose a secular education that makes little or no reference to religion and thereby, in their view, implies that religion is misguided or at least unimportant.

1. Government–Sponsored Religious Exercises

The modern Court has consistently ruled that government may not conduct religious exercises in the public schools. The landmark decision of *Engel v. Vitale* (S.Ct.1962) held that the Establishment Clause was violated by a practice of having public school students recite aloud a short prayer, composed by the state school board, in the classroom at the beginning of each school day. The prayer, which was intended to be non-denominational in nature, read: "Almighty God, we acknowledge our dependence upon thee, and we beg thy blessings upon us, our parents, our teachers, and our country." In the next term, *Abington School District v. Schempp* (S.Ct.1963) struck down the daily practice of having teachers or students select and read Bible verses in the classroom or over the school intercom.

As noted in Chapter 1, *Engel* and *Schempp* together rejected two readings of the Establishment Clause that would have permitted some government-sponsored religious exercises in schools. First, the generality and non-denominational nature of the New York prayer did not, the *Engel* Court said, save it from invalidation. *Schempp* explicitly agreed that the Establishment Clause prohibits more than just preference for one religion over others. Government must be "neutral" between religion and non-religion as well; the same concern for the conscience of minority religious adherents extends to those who follow no faith at all.

Second, the Court rejected the states' arguments that the prayers and Bible readings should be upheld because objecting students were free to remain silent or leave the room. In both cases, the Court ruled that the Establishment Clause forbids government to set up an official religion, or to exercise power over religious matters, even if government does not coerce citizens to follow the preferred faith. The government must be neutral toward religion. This proposition did not appear necessary to decide the particular case, for the Court also stated that the prayers and Bible readings, in the context of the school classroom, did place "indirect coercive pressure" on students of minority views. The broader language indicated a flat ban on government-conducted religious exercises in public schools.

The Court continues to struggle, both in public school cases and in other cases, with the question whether the Establishment Clause forbids even non-coercive religious statements or practices by government. Currently the justices are deeply divided between those who think that only coercive government practices are forbidden and those who think that government may not "endorse" religion even in non-coercive ways. (See Chapter 1, as well as part B of this chapter, for further discussion.)

In terms of underlying Religion Clause values, those who would permit non-coercive endorsements of religion say that religious liberty is the primary value and that it is not infringed when no person is coerced to participate in a religious practice. They also point out that government may espouse other views—from democracy to free-market capitalism— so that to forbid it from espousing religion is to treat religion unequally. On the other hand, *Engel* and *Schempp*'s principle that government may not conduct even non-coercive religious exercises rests on the value of church-state separation, as well as on a broad understanding of religious liberty under which government should not try to affect people's religious views even by means short of coercion. Defenders of *Engel* and *Schempp* also point out that the content of any official prayer or religious ritual is bound to be that of a particular faith or group of faiths, and thus will treat other faiths unequally.

The prayer and Bible reading decisions produced widespread public opposition. Many proposals have been introduced in Congress to overturn the decisions by constitutional amendment or to strip the

Court of jurisdiction over school prayer cases. But none of these proposals has succeeded, and the Court has adhered to the decisions.

In *Engel*, Justice Black's majority opinion focused on the history of conflict over attempts by the state to write or prescribe particular prayers or liturgies (for example, English disputes over the content of the officially-approved Book of Common Prayer). From these episodes, the Court concluded that "it is no part of the business of government to compose official prayers for any group of the American people to recite as part of a religious program carried on by government." But *Schempp* showed that the government's composition of the prayer was not (in the Court's view) the constitutional wrong, for *Schempp* struck down school-initiated Bible readings even when students chose the passages.

Several other important contentions concerning school-sponsored religious exercises were rejected in *Schempp*. The Court dismissed claims that such exercises actually serve the Religion Clause principles of free exercise and nonestablishment. Both the state and Justice Stewart's dissent argued that students who are required to attend several hours of school each day have a free exercise interest in expressing their faith in that setting. The Court responded that the Free Exercise Clause "has never meant that a majority could use the machinery of the State to practice its beliefs." (Left unexplored was the extent to which individuals could practice or express their religion in the public schools without using state machinery.)

The Court also rejected the argument that without official religious exercises, "a 'religion of secularism' is established in the schools." The majority said that although the government could not establish secularism "in the sense of affirmatively opposing or showing hostility to religion," the barring of official exercises did not have such an effect. The principle of neutrality allowed plenty of room, the Court suggested, for including the study of the Bible or comparative religion "objectively as part of a secular program of education." Justice Goldberg, concurring, added that schools could and should avoid a "brooding and pervasive devotion to the secular" by a curriculum that included "teaching **about** religion, as distinguished from the teaching **of** religion" (emphasis in original).

Then in turn the Court rejected the argument that the Bible readings could simply be seen as such an objective exercise—as instruction, for example, in moral values, great literature, or Western history. The "pervading religious character of the ceremony [wa]s evident" from the fact that either the King James (Protestant) or Douay (Catholic) versions of the Bible were specifically authorized for readings, apparently in order to respect the religious sensibilities of the majority of students, and that objectors were allowed to opt out of attending.

The Court extended this reasoning in holding, years later, that the display of the Ten Commandments in public school classrooms could not be justified on the basis that the commandments constituted "the fundamental legal code of Western Civilization." *Stone v. Graham* (S.Ct.1980) (per curiam). In a brief opinion applying the by-then-familiar test of *Lemon v. Kurtzman* (S.Ct.1971), the Court said that while discussing the commandments in the curriculum would serve an educational function, posting them on the wall instead encouraged students to "meditate upon, perhaps to venerate and obey," them. The "pre-eminent" purpose and effect of the display was religious, not secular.

Finally, as discussed in greater detail shortly, the Court held that even a statute that authorized a moment of silent, as opposed to vocal or collective, prayer was unconstitutional. *Wallace v. Jaffree* (S.Ct.1985). The Court said that because a preexisting statute had authorized students to take a moment of silence for "meditation," the addition of the phrase " . . . or voluntary prayer" in the new statute, the one being challenged, had the purpose and effect of favoring prayer.

As we have said, this line of decisions rested on the principle of church-state separation and the notion that government could and should remain neutral toward religion by not becoming involved with it. But if government is forbidden even to make general, non-coercive religious statements, what would that mean for a host of other religious elements in government? Village or school Christmas celebrations, religious art in state museums, prayers at inaugurals and other public events, references to God in the Declaration of Independence or the speeches of Abraham Lincoln, and numerous other religious elements are a part of America's history and traditions. If such practices are unconstitutional, is the real role of religion in American culture being artificially suppressed—so that government becomes hostile to religion rather than neutral?

Although we will discuss this question later as well, it is worth noting some distinctions that have been offered by various justices. First, as *Schempp* itself stated, the government is free to teach about religion in an objective manner as long as it does not promote or celebrate it. Second, some religious references by government could be seen as simple acknowledgements of the role of religion in culture: religious paintings or masses in art or music classes or in state museums, or perhaps (more controversially) a school Christmas program or display that includes religious symbols or songs. Finally, some justices have suggested that certain official prayers or slogans with a general theistic content, such as the motto "In God We Trust" on coins, have come to lose any real religious meaning and serve simply as solemn or patriotic statements. See, e.g., *Schempp* (Brennan, J., concurring); *Lynch v. Donnelly* (S.Ct.1984) (O'Connor, J., concurring). Commentators often refer to such mild forms of official religion as "civil religion" or "ceremonial deism." Notably, many of these practices occur outside the context of public schools, and hence the Court appears to be more tolerant of them (see part B).

By the early 1990s, critics of the school prayer and Bible-reading rulings had reason to hope that they might be overturned or limited. With the appointment of several judicial "conservatives" to the Court, the separation and neutrality approaches of *Lemon* had increasingly fallen into question. But to the surprise of many, *Lee v. Weisman* (S.Ct.1992) largely reaffirmed the ban on government-conducted religious exercises in schools, in holding that officials at a junior high school could not invite a clergyman to give opening and closing prayers as part of the school's official graduation ceremony. Although the clergyman, a rabbi, composed the prayer himself, the principal gave him guidelines and advised that the prayers should be "nonsectarian."

The majority opinion (written by Justice Kennedy, to the chagrin of many conservatives) did not decide the continuing question of whether noncoercive religious exercises were permissible. The Court noted that "at a minimum" the Establishment Clause forbids coerced religious practices, and it found such coercion in this case. The school's action placed "public pressure, as well as peer pressure," on students "to stand as a group or, at least, maintain respectful silence" during the prayers, acts that could reasonably be construed as showing support for their content. The pressure was not eliminated by the fact that attendance at the graduation ceremony was legally voluntary, unlike the compulsory classes where the *Engel* and *Schempp* exercises occurred. "Law reaches past formalism," Justice Kennedy said, and graduation is a significant enough event that the state may not "exact religious conformity from a student as the price of attending" it.

Justice Scalia's dissent attacked the Court's notion of "peer pressure" coercion, pointing out that standing in silence during a speech can reflect simple politeness and not approval of what is said. (The majority had recognized this but had emphasized that actions in school ceremonies were more sensitive and open to misinterpretation than actions in other contexts.) Scalia argued that the Establishment Clause should be limited to coercion "by force of law or threat of penalty," lest a whole host of traditional pronouncements by government be deemed unconstitutional. If a school cannot conduct a prayer because it is inherently coercive, Scalia asked, is it also forbidden to conduct the Pledge of Allegiance, since the government may not coerce political affirmations any more than religious affirmations?

Let us leave aside for a moment the question whether the Establishment Clause should be read to forbid non-coercive statements by government. Justice Scalia did have a point when he suggested that *Weisman*'s concept of improper coercion is so expansive that it really amounts to a reaffirmation of the ban on any government-conducted religious exercises, even non-coercive ones, in the public schools. (An exception might be prayers at a nonrequired school event that is arguably less significant than a high school graduation. Cf. *Ingebretsen v. Jackson School District* (5th Cir.1996) (prayers at high school football games and other events; *Tanford v. Brand* (7th Cir.1997) (invocation at university graduation)). In some passages, *Weisman* does suggest that government may not engage in religious speech, however non-coercive the speech is: "In religious debate or expression [unlike political debate] the government is not a prime participant, for the Framers deemed religious establishment antithetical to the freedom of all."

In addition to rejecting a coercion standard that would give government leeway to sponsor religion, *Weisman* also adhered to *Engel* and *Schempp* in rejecting the argument that the rabbi's prayer should be permitted because it was "nonsectarian" and embraced the entire "Judaeo–Christian tradition." The Court noted that even a nonsectarian official religion violated the principle "protect[ing] religion from governmental interference" and concluded: "The suggestion that government may establish an official or civic religion as a means of avoiding the establishment of a religion with more specific creeds strikes us as a contradiction that cannot be accepted."

But the constitutional issues concerning religious expression in public schools—including some of the free speech and free exercise interests that affect the analysis—are by no means exhausted by these decisions.

2. Privately–Initiated Religious Activity

Another line of decisions, beginning in the 1980s, made increasingly clear that religious activity need not be barred from public schools—and indeed in many instances could not constitutionally be barred—when such activity was initiated and conducted by private individuals rather than by the government. Preserving room for private religious activity reflects the principle, emphasized in Chapter 3, that the religious expression and activity of citizens are highly protected by both the Free Speech and Free Exercise clauses. Thus, the overriding question is whether the religious activity is "state action" (government action) or not. See *Board of Education v. Mergens* (S.Ct.1990) (noting the "crucial" difference between religious speech by government and by private citizens).

The Court first held that when a state university permits a wide range of student-initiated groups to meet in campus buildings, it not only may but **must** permit a student religious group to meet on the same terms. *Widmar v. Vincent* (S.Ct.1981). When the University of Missouri disallowed an evangelical Christian student group's meeting on the ground that it was religious, it engaged in a form of discrimination that was barred by the Free Speech Clause and was not required by the Establishment Clause.

First, the Court applied general principles of free speech analysis and held that by permitting many student groups to meet, the university had made its property a "public forum" for student speech, analogous to a street or park where citizens may freely speak. Exclusion of the religious group constituted discrimination based on the content of the group's expression, which is impermissible unless it is "necessary to serve a compelling interest and ... is narrowly drawn to achieve that end."

Furthermore, the denial of the Christian group's meeting was not justified by the need to obey the Establishment Clause. Applying the *Lemon* test, the Court held that once many groups were allowed to meet, the inclusion of religious groups would not have the effect of approving or favoring religion— "at least in the absence of empirical evidence that religious groups will dominate [the] open forum." The distinction from the cases of government-sponsored prayers or Bible readings was plain (although *Widmar* never mentioned those decisions): if the religious students met, the university would merely be permitting their expression and not sponsoring it.

In a final important principle, *Widmar* added that the state could not assert a compelling interest in preserving a stricter separation of church and state mandated by the Missouri state constitution. The state rule could not overcome the interests protected by the federal Free Speech and Free Exercise clauses.

The principles of *Widmar* can be seen as protecting religious equality and liberty against the most rigid version of church-state separation. Exclusion of the evangelical group would treat religious speech differently from other speech and would restrict the evangelical students' ability to practice their faith fully by meeting on campus. The only principle that could defend the exclusion is a notion of separation so broad that it deems any religious activity improper in public institutions. Such a view would impose very serious costs to religious equality and liberty. Moreover, even exclusion of the religious group would require some government involvement: as the Court noted, the university would have to define when a group's speech became "religious" and therefore subject to exclusion.

After *Widmar*, the question arose whether its principles applied to high schools, to protect student religious clubs against being excluded from meeting on the same terms as other clubs. Some courts and commentators answered no: they reasoned that high school club programs were not the same kind of wide-open expressive forum as is a college campus, and that high school students were more impressionable and likely to view a religious club as school-endorsed. But Congress disagreed and in 1984 passed the Equal Access Act (EAA), which states that any high school receiving federal funds that has an "open forum" for student clubs may not deny a club permission to meet because of the "religious, political, philosophical, or other content of the speech at such meetings." 20 U.S.C.A. § 4071. The Supreme Court upheld the EAA against constitutional challenge in *Board of Education v. Mergens, supra.*

Since the students who sought to meet in *Mergens* relied on their statutory rights, the Court did not consider whether they also had constitutional rights under *Widmar*. First, the Court held that the protections of the Equal Access Act applied even if the list of student clubs was not so wide-ranging as to create a "public forum" along the lines of the college campus in *Widmar*. Although the EAA is generally based on *Widmar*'s constitutional principles, its definition of an "open forum" for student groups is broader than the constitutional definition: the EAA is triggered as soon as the school permits "one or more noncurriculum related student groups" to meet. 20 U.S.C.A. § 4071(b). The statute governed, the Court said, because the school district permitted groups that were not "directly related" to the curriculum, such as chess, scuba diving, and service clubs.

The Court then applied the principles of *Widmar* to hold that inclusion of the student club did not violate the Establishment Clause. Writing for four justices, Justice O'Connor emphasized the "crucial difference" between government speech and private speech and said that permitting the latter did not constitute a government endorsement of religion. She argued that high school students were sufficiently mature to understand the difference between permission and endorsement, and that exclusion of the club would in fact show hostility to religion. In addition, two justices who reject the "endorsement" test in favor of a more lenient "noncoercion" test, Scalia and Kennedy, easily found that permitting the religious club did not coerce any students to join it.

Two more separationist justices, Brennan and Marshall, concurred in the result but more narrowly. They warned that because the school district gave official approval to all clubs and deemed them part of its educational mission, students under such circumstances might perceive an endorsement of the religious club. Thus the school had to "affirmatively disclaim[ ] any endorsement of the Christian Club." Although these views were not necessary to the *Mergens* result, if lower courts give them any weight there may be continued litigation over whether the nature of the club program in a given case involves school endorsement.

The Equal Access Act teaches several lessons about religious freedom. It shows that sometimes the legislature, not the judiciary, takes the lead in protecting liberties. It is also noteworthy while the impetus for the EAA was the exclusion of religious clubs, its proponents had to extend protection to political and philosophical views in order to secure passage and satisfy the constitutional standard of government neutrality between religious speech and speech expressing other ideas. The results may be dramatic, as Justice Stevens pointed out in his lone dissent: if a school wants to have any extracurricular clubs it must be prepared to allow some highly controversial ones. Schools are permitted to deny clubs that would "materially" interfere with school activities or that are directed by "nonschool persons." 20 U.S.C.A. § 4071(c). (Could a school reject a student Ku Klux Klan club, or a Satanist club, on any of these grounds?)

Permitting equal access to student religious clubs may generally promote both equality and liberty while maintaining church-state separation; but these three values could still collide in some of the details. For example, the Act provides that no teacher may be a sponsor of the religious club—even though teachers may sponsor other clubs—or do anything more than serve as a nonparticipating monitor at its meetings. While this treats religious clubs unequally, it arguably is necessary to avoid any subtle religious pressure on students by teachers. The restriction could be seen as serving the values of both liberty and separation.

Some issues concerning student clubs remain unresolved. While the Equal Access Act does not apply to elementary schools, it has been claimed that the First Amendment itself prohibits a school from barring an elementary-level club solely because it is religious. Courts have divided on the question: some apply the equal access principle, but others say that no school in those lower grades can have a truly open forum or truly student-initiated clubs.

Another emerging question is whether schools may deny access to a religious club on the ground that it engages in religious "discrimination" by requiring its officers or members to be adherents of the faith. One court of appeals held that a school policy forbidding discrimination by clubs could be applied to the offices of secretary and activities coordinator in a religious club, but not to the offices of president, vice-president, and music director. *Hsu v. Roslyn Free School District* (2d Cir.1996). Again, the terms of the Equal Access Act itself may not resolve all such situations, but the religious clubs assert a First Amendment right to require commitments of faith from their officers and members. They argue that otherwise they are being discriminated against, because other ideological clubs are free to require such commitments (for example, a student environmental club may require students to express interest in saving the environment).

The principle of equal freedom for religious speech was again evident in the Court's ruling that when a school district opened its buildings after hours to use by outside groups for "social" or "civic" purposes, it could not refuse access to an evangelical church that planned to show a series of films on family and child-rearing. *Lamb's Chapel v. Center Moriches School District* (S.Ct.1993). Again the discriminatory refusal violated the Free Speech Clause and was not justified by the Establishment Clause.

Most importantly, *Lamb's Chapel* held that the denial of access violated the Free Speech Clause even if the school had not created a wide-ranging public forum by opening its facilities. Under free speech law, even if the government creates only a limited, "nonpublic" forum for discussion of a specific topic, it cannot discriminate among differing viewpoints on that topic. The school district's policy permitted meetings for "social" or "civic" purposes; the church's series on family values fit that category and could not be excluded simply because its viewpoint on those subjects was religious.

Based on similar principles, the Court in *Rosenberger v. Rector of University of Virginia* (S.Ct.1995) held that the university had engaged in impermissible viewpoint discrimination when it gave financial assistance to a wide range of student publications but withheld funding from a Christian student magazine. The basis for denying funds was that the magazine "promote[d] or manifest[ed] a particular belie[f] in or about a deity or an ultimate reality." The university argued that this exclusion did not discriminate on the basis of viewpoint, because it covered atheistic as well as theistic publications. The university said it was merely leaving out the "subject matter" of religion. But the Court majority still saw the policy as viewpoint-based: it excluded two viewpoints (atheism and theism) but funded publications reflecting many other perspectives. The Christian magazine wrote on the same topics—cultural, moral, and political issues—as were written on by other student publications that received funding.

Both *Lamb's Chapel* and *Rosenberger* hold that to deny a group access because its perspective is religious is an exclusion of a certain viewpoint (or viewpoints) on many topics: it is not simply an exclusion of a certain limited topic called "religion." In practice, this logic makes it much easier for religious groups to obtain access to government facilities. They need not show that the government has created a wide-ranging forum, because viewpoint discrimination is prohibited no matter what the forum: they need only show that their activity or expression fits within the topic of whatever forum the government has created.

These holdings do not likely mean that a given form of religious expression must always be permitted whenever a number of other forms of expression are permitted—for government has discretion to define its forum in religion-neutral terms, and a particular kind of religious expression may not fit within the forum. For example, that a school schedules an afterschool period for student clubs does not mean that a church group must be allowed to hold meetings during that hour. And had the school district in *Lamb's Chapel* opened its rooms solely for community groups discussing "school-related" issues, it probably would not have to permit a church service or prayer meeting. A more controversial application of this principle is a recent ruling that a school district that opened its rooms for general civic purposes could refuse to allow a church service. *Bronx Household of Faith v. Community School District No. 10* (2d Cir.1997).

On an even more controversial matter, *Rosenberger* extended the principle of equal treatment for religious groups to the situation of government financial assistance. The majority held that including religious publications in the university's general funding program would not violate the Establishment Clause, primarily because such a policy would show neutrality rather than favoritism toward religion. But as is discussed in greater detail in Chapter 5 (on government funding), the majority wrote narrowly on this issue. For example, it distinguished this situation, where the university paid the bills incurred by student magazines, from one "where the government makes direct money payments to sectarian institutions."

3. Drawing the Line Between Government and Private Religious Activity

The distinction between the religious activity of government and of individual citizens, while crucial, is not always easy to make. Because government owns public school property and schedules and oversees activities in the school, even ensuring that student-initiated religious activity can proceed freely will require some government involvement. For example, even to permit student religious groups to meet on the same terms as other groups requires providing them with rooms, utilities such as heat and electricity, and perhaps access to school media. But at what point does making religious activity possible on government property cross over into government sponsorship of religious activity?

The simplest case is when government makes religious speech or activity possible on the same terms as other activities—as it did in the "open forum" cases discussed in the previous section (*Widmar* through *Rosenberger*). Another possible example of that principle is the so-called moment of silence policy. Under this, students in the classroom are given a moment at the beginning of each day to engage silently in reflection or, if they choose, prayer.

As noted above (part A–1), the Supreme Court has struck down a statute providing for a moment of silence, but the reasoning could be taken as very limited. *Wallace v. Jaffree, supra.* Alabama already had a statute authorizing a moment of silence "for meditation," which was conceded to be valid. Then a new statute was passed authorizing a silent moment "for meditation or voluntary prayer." The Court reasoned that the previous statute already allowed silent prayer (as a kind of meditation), so the only reason for adding " . . . or voluntary prayer" was to encourage students to engage in prayer over other forms of reflection. The Court bolstered this conclusion with statements by the new law's sponsor that his only goal was to "to return voluntary prayer to our public schools."

But *Jaffree* suggests that the Court would uphold some moment-of-silence statutes that did not have the Alabama law's unusual history. As Justice O'Connor argued in a concurring opinion, a moment of silence, if fairly designed and implemented, does not encourage prayer over other activity and (unlike vocal prayer or Bible readings) does not force other students to listen. It thus arguably respects the values of both religious equality and liberty. *Jaffree* seemed to accept the constitutionality of the original law authorizing "meditation," under which students could pray. See also *Bown v. Gwinnett County Schools* (11th Cir.1997) (upholding another such law). Even a law that authorized "meditation or voluntary prayer" might pass muster if the court were less suspicious of the legislative intent. In actual practice some teachers would encourage students to pray, but those particular abuses could be challenged without striking down the law in general.

More difficult questions are presented when a school singles out religion for concern but assertedly does so simply to accommodate individual religious exercise. Early in the modern era of Religion Clause decisions, the Court confronted a pair of "release time" programs under which students were let out of school to attend religious education classes taught by local clergy. The asserted goal was to keep the school schedule from crowding out children's opportunities for religious development. The Court struck down such a program where the religion classes were held in the public school buildings. *McCollum v. Board of Education* (S.Ct.1948). But only four years later, it turned around and upheld a second program, saying it was different because the classes were off school grounds. *Zorach v. Clauson* (S.Ct.1952).

The essence of the constitutional wrong in *McCollum* seemed to be that the state was using its "compulsory public school machinery" to encourage attendance at the religion classes. Students who chose not to attend the classes had to remain at school in study hall (Justice Jackson, in *Zorach*, called it "a temporary jail for a pupil who will not go to Church"); and the school kept records of those who did attend the classes. (The same factors may have been present in *Zorach*, although the opinions are somewhat unclear on the matter.)

The *Zorach* Court's ground of distinction between the two cases—classes on versus off campus—is unsatisfying because it has little to do with this legal wrong. The release time program could be used to pressure students to attend religion classes off campus just as much as on. Conversely, if the school simply dismissed all students early so that some could attend religion classes, there would not seem to be favoritism for religion even if the school allowed the religion classes to be conducted in its own buildings.

Whether or not the two cases were distinguishable factually, the two majority opinions present sharply contrasting general approaches to Religion Clause adjudication. *McCollum* emphasized the value of church-state separation, asserting that the wall "must be kept high and impregnable." It disapproved of the "close cooperation" between school and churches "in promoting religious education." But in *Zorach*, Justice Douglas for the majority wrote that the First Amendment "does not say that in every and all respects there shall be a separation of Church and State." Rather, "We are a religious people whose institutions presuppose a Supreme Being.... When the state encourages religious instruction or cooperates with religious authorities in adjusting the schedule of public events to sectarian needs, it follows in the best of our traditions." To forbid such accommodations "would show a callous indifference to religious groups." Thus *Zorach* sounded the theme of religious liberty: religious practice is a good thing, and government was welcome to facilitate such practice as long as it did not coerce anyone to participate. The shift in approaches came partly because new justices were appointed, but also because others (including Douglas himself) changed their position.

Another uncertain line between government-sponsored and privately-initiated religion has appeared in the wake of *Lee v. Weisman*'s invalidation of a school-initiated prayer at graduation ceremonies (see part A–1). While prayers controlled by school officials are clearly unconstitutional, in other situations a prayer in the ceremony would be much closer to simple free speech. Suppose, for example, that the class president or valedictorian, allowed to compose her own speech, includes in it a prayer or a religious testimony without any school involvement. But see *Guidry v. Calcasieu Parish School Board* (E.D.La.1989) (forbidding such a speech).

A major current controversy is whether prayers at graduation are constitutional if the decision to have them is made by a student vote (usually of the majority of the graduating class) rather than by school officials, and the prayer is composed and given by a student without school involvement. Federal courts of appeals have split over the question. Cf. *Jones v. Clear Creek School District* (5th Cir.1993) (approving such prayers) with *ACLU v. Black Horse Pike Board of Education* (3d Cir.1996) (en banc) (striking them down). Defenders of such prayers say that the fact that it is the student body that decides whether and how to pray removes the elements of official involvement and approval that made the prayer in *Weisman* unconstitutional. Opponents argue that even a student-initiated prayer in official exercises amounts to government-imposed majority religion; that it is still school policy that authorizes a prayer; and that school officials cannot evade constitutional limits by delegating the decision to the student majority.

4. Religion and the School Curriculum

Although much attention has focused on school ceremonies such as graduation services or morning classroom exercises, the primary way in which public schools influence students is through the everyday curriculum. The content of the curriculum has posed a variety of First Amendment issues. Generally the state has wide discretion to choose the contents of the curriculum according to educational judgments; but that discretion has been limited by the First Amendment.

The bar on government-sponsored religious exercises (set forth in *Engel* and *Schempp*) seems to entail that teachers may not espouse or promote religious doctrine in their classes either. For example, under the principles of those decisions a high school biology teacher could not teach students that the book of Genesis is the correct account of the origins of life. The reasons are the same as the reasons for prohibiting prayers or Bible readings: a teacher's statements can put great pressure on dissenting students, and make them feel like second-class members of the group, even if they are technically free to express disagreement with the teacher's views.

On the other hand, the question may be more difficult at the college level, where professors commonly express their personal views on the subject matter of their courses and students are presumably more mature and less likely to be indoctrinated by a teacher's opinions. Can a biology professor at a state university make non-coercive expressions of his belief that all organisms were created by God? See *Bishop v. Aronov* (11th Cir.1991) (upholding reprimand of physiology professor for making religious statements in class and offering additional sessions on his religious views; rejecting professor's claimed right of academic freedom).

In any event, the Court has gone further to shield the curriculum from religious influences than simply forbidding teachers to teach religious doctrines as true. For example, an Arkansas statute that barred the teaching of evolution in state schools (enacted shortly after the famous Scopes "monkey" trial) was struck down forty years later on the ground that it lacked a secular purpose. *Epperson v. Arkansas* (S.Ct.1968). The Court noted the state's general power to prescribe the school curriculum. But, it said, there was "no suggestion" that the anti-evolution law was motivated or justified by any policy other than the "fundamentalist sectarian conviction" of many citizens.

In the years after *Epperson*, religious opponents of evolution developed a theory called "scientific creationism," which they presented as an alternative explanation of origins. They claimed that scientific evidence refuted evolution and supported divine creation. Adopting a new legal strategy, they secured "balanced treatment" laws requiring that scientific creationism be taught whenever evolution was. But the Court struck down Louisiana's version of the law, again on the basis that it lacked a secular purpose. *Edwards v. Aguillard* (S.Ct.1987).

Justice Brennan's majority opinion dismissed as a "sham" the state's asserted purposes of securing academic freedom and making science teaching more "comprehensive." The law was unnecessary because teachers were already free to question evolution or present evidence for other theories. Moreover, the law singled out creationism as the only theory of origins to received balanced treatment. The Court also pointed to statements by the sponsoring legislator, who expressed his "disdain" for evolution and his hope that the law would benefit his own religious views.

In *Epperson*, and perhaps in *Aguillard* as well, the Court went beyond preventing the explicit teaching of religious views. It may be argued that the "balanced treatment" statute in *Aguillard* was unconstitutional because creationism is not really a scientific theory, but a religious doctrine, which state schools may not endorse as true. (But suppose the creationist theory makes no reference to God or a divine being but simply says that species appeared suddenly as if created?) However, this argument cannot explain *Epperson*, where the state did not teach religion but merely removed a secular theory from the curriculum. Justice Black, concurring in *Epperson*'s result but disagreeing with the reasoning, thought that the removal of evolution served the legitimate secular purpose of keeping the curriculum neutral as to controversial subjects.

Both decisions have been criticized on the ground that they use the religious motivation of legislators as evidence of unconstitutionality. Critics argue that if legislators voted for a civil rights bill and explained they were doing it because "God created all men equal," the law should not and would not be held invalid. But as will be discussed later (Chapter 6), the Court has not often engaged in such scrutiny of legislators' actual motivations.

Despite the Court's arguments against religious teaching in the curriculum, the absence of such teaching concerns many people. Does it teach students the lesson that religious ideas are unimportant, and reflect the "brooding and pervasive devotion to the secular" that Justice Goldberg warned about in *Schempp*? The issue is not merely theoretical but real, and relevant to educational quality as well. A 1980s survey of textbooks found that religious influences on American history were often ignored or downplayed; "pilgrims," for example, were defined as "people who travel to other lands." One attempt to solve this problem is to teach students objectively about religious history and religious thought, as the Court suggested in *Schempp*. Such teaching can occur either by conducting separate religious studies courses or by studying religious ideas and influences in connection with other courses such as literature, history, or science. Efforts to present such objective teaching continue today across the nation.

Opponents of secular-oriented school curriculums have pursued legal avenues but have had little success. One strategy has been to try to get elements of the current curriculums declared as a religion—the religion of "secular humanism"—and therefore banned from the schools. In Mobile, Alabama, a group of parents sued to enjoin the use of 44 textbooks in home economics and social science courses, claiming that the books taught moral relativism and ignored the role of religion in American life. The federal district court ruled that the books did teach the religion of secular humanism, which the court noted had been listed as a religion in a footnote in an earlier Supreme Court decision, *Torcaso v. Watkins* (see Chapter 7).

The court of appeals, however, ruled that even if secular humanism were a religion for purposes of the Establishment Clause, none of the challenged books endorsed such a creed. *Smith v. Board of Commissioners of Mobile County Schools* (11th Cir. 1987). The court said that the books merely taught values such as independent thought, tolerance of others, and logical reasoning, which were not in opposition to religion; indeed, many of the books specifically acknowledged that religion is one source of moral values. And if the books omitted religious influences in history, this at most made them educationally inadequate, a matter within the schools' discretion. The court hearkened back to Justice Jackson's warning in *McCollum v. Board of Education* that "[i]f we are to eliminate everything that is objectionable to any of [America's] warring sects or inconsistent with any of their doctrines, we will leave public education in shreds."

A somewhat less disruptive proposal by religious parents is to remove their children from objectionable classes and programs, rather than have the programs banned. Here, too, however, the parents' legal theories have been unsuccessful. A group of "born again" Christian parents and children in Tennessee objected to an elementary school reading series. They believed the children must not be exposed to references to mental telepathy, which they characterized as "occult practices"; to evolution and feminism, which contradicted their beliefs in a literal interpretation of the book of Genesis and in traditional women's roles; and to various forms of "secular humanist" reasoning. They asked that the children be excused and given alternative reading assignments. The school board at first agreed, then after a few months changed its mind. The plaintiffs sued and won a district court order upholding their right to "opt out." Again, however, the court of appeals reversed. *Mozert v. Hawkins County Board of Education* (6th Cir.1987).

The parents invoked the Free Exercise Clause, claiming that the school had compelled their children to read materials that their religious beliefs forbade them to read. To challenge the government's asserted need to assign the objectionable materials, the parents pointed out that the children had read alternative books for several months. But the court of appeals ruled against the plaintiffs on the first part of the free exercise analysis: their religious exercise had not been "burdened." The students had been compelled only to read the books, not to assent or express assent to anything in them: the court rejected, without giving much explanation, the plaintiffs' claim that mere exposure to the books was enough to violate their religious tenets. (A concurring judge disagreed on this point, noting that for centuries the Roman Catholic Church had maintained an index of books that Catholics were forbidden to read.) *Yoder* was distinguished on the ground that the plaintiffs had not claimed that going to school in the first place conflicted with their faith.

Another concurring judge added that the schools also had a compelling interest in denying such opt outs. These interests included (1) "teaching students how to think critically," (2) "avoiding the religious divisiveness" that would follow from excusing some students, and (3) avoiding setting a precedent for other opt-outs that together would seriously disrupt the curriculum.

The court of appeals decisions in *Smith* and *Mozert* suggest that parents who object on religious grounds to the contents of the curriculum will not be able to raise Religion Clause claims. If these parents are unsuccessful in affecting the curriculum politically through electing school officials, they may move in larger numbers to private religious

schools and push for financial assistance to such
schools (see Chapter 5).

B. RELIGIOUS ELEMENTS IN OTHER
GOVERNMENT ACTIVITIES

Although most Supreme Court cases about religious elements in government institutions have concerned the public schools, the issue naturally arises
in a host of other contexts as well. The general
principles in the two areas are the same; however,
the Court has been more inclined to accept government-sponsored religious elements in these other
contexts than in the schools. The previous section
discussed the Court's "special sensitivity" to state
imposition of religion in the schools. But the justices appear to be somewhat less willing to try to
disentangle religion from public displays and ceremonies in the myriad of other situations. Thus
there is more room for the kind of relatively general, mild religious practices that are often referred to
as "civil religion" or "ceremonial deism."

Some constitutional principles are similar in and
out of the school context. To begin with, it seems
clear that religious speech by private citizens is
protected on other forms of government property
just as it is in public schools. In a number of
relatively early cases, the Court established that
Jehovah's Witnesses could not be refused permission to preach in city streets or parks because of
opposition to their inflammatory messages and be-

liefs. See, e.g., *Niemotko v. Maryland* (S.Ct.1951); *Fowler v. Rhode Island* (S.Ct.1953).

Recently the Court reaffirmed the principle of equal freedom for religious speech in holding that the Ku Klux Klan could not be refused permission to erect a free-standing cross in a public plaza where other groups had been permitted to erect displays. *Capitol Square Review and Advisory Board v. Pinette* (S.Ct.1995). The state of Ohio, which ran the plaza because it surrounded the state capitol building, had denied the Klan a permit not because the display's content was racist or would incite violence, but because it was religious. The Court held that since parks and squares are "traditional" public forums for citizen expression, the exclusion of religious expression was unconstitutional unless there was a compelling reason for it. (Although the Klan's speech is often purely political, here the fact that it took the form of displaying a cross made it religious.)

Relying on schools cases such as *Lamb's Chapel* and *Widmar*, the Court held that exclusion of private parties' religious speech was not justified by the Establishment Clause. Four justices stated that such citizen speech in a public forum could never constitute an establishment. But three others applied the "endorsement" test and would examine each case to determine whether, in the particular circumstances, a reasonable observer might think the government endorsed the display. They warned that an unattended display in front of the capitol could appear to have been erected by the state, unlike the situation where citizens could be seen manning a display or attending a rally. But these justices ultimately found no state endorsement in *Pinette* itself, because the cross was in a place used by other private groups and it carried a sign disclaiming any such endorsement.

The more difficult and controversial issues have involved religious content in expression by the government itself, rather than by private citizens. The Court has allowed more government-sponsored religious activity outside of the public schools than it has in the schools—although it has struck down some such forms of activity. In taking a more lenient approach to the public square generally, the Court may have been influenced by at least two factors. First, adults are less likely overall to be pressured or influenced by governmental religious pronouncements than are children who are exposed to such pronouncements in the confined atmosphere of a public school.

Second, although removing all traditional religious elements from government ceremonies and statements is difficult enough even in the schools, it is even more difficult to do across the whole range of governmental actions. This has been an uncomfortable question for the justices—as is exemplified by the fact that even as the Court continues to decide whether certain governmental religious statements are permissible, it opens its own sessions with the cry of "God save the United States and this honorable Court."

Early on, the "wall of separation" metaphor and the decisions disapproving even noncoercive religious exercises in schools suggested that official exercises outside the school context would be forbidden too. But then the Court upheld the practice of prayers in state legislatures under a diametrically opposite approach, relying heavily on the fact that the practice had been engaged in by the first Congress. *Marsh v. Chambers* (S.Ct.1983). (Note the contrast with the invalidation of prayers in schools.)

Nebraska's legislature opened each legislative day with a prayer by a state-paid chaplain, a position that had been filled for nearly 20 years by the same Presbyterian minister. As Justice Brennan's dissent argued, the practice could not survive the *Lemon v. Kurtzman* test or its underlying principles of separation and neutrality: the prayers were official acts of worship, not merely acknowledgements that many Americans hold religious beliefs. But the Court relied on the "unique history" of the practice, pointing out that only three days before Congress adopted the language of the Religion Clauses in 1789, it authorized appointment of a paid chaplain to lead prayers, a policy that has continued ever since. The Court could not believe that the delegates "intended the Establishment Clause to forbid what they had just declared acceptable."

Marsh reflects a particularly aggressive use of "original intent" in constitutional interpretation: the Court relied on the founders' unexamined acceptance of a particular practice to validate it, rather than using the historical record to develop a legal principle that could then be applied to the facts. The decision thus implicates the general questions about whether the founders' intent should govern the meaning of the Constitution (for a brief discussion, see Chapter 1). Is such a rule necessary to keep the Constitution from changing into whatever a majority of justices think it should be? Or would limiting the Constitution to the founders' specific intent prevent it from serving as our foundational document as circumstances change over time—for example, as American society becomes much more religiously diverse?

Because *Marsh* looked to specific historical practice rather than general principles, it is hard to apply the decision to other situations. For example, an Alabama state judge recently sparked nationwide controversy by beginning his court sessions with prayers and posting the Ten Commandments directly behind his bench. Do judicial prayers fit within the historical example of legislative prayers approved in *Marsh*? Might a judge be different because his prayers place pressures, however subtle, on the litigants, jurors, and lawyers in his courtroom?

Setting aside *Marsh*'s reliance on history, the different results concerning prayer in legislatures and schools might be explained if the Court employed a "noncoercion" test across the board for Establishment Clause cases. The Court could say that official exercises in the schools inherently put pressure on impressionable children—but that (as

Marsh itself noted) legislators as adults are not subject to the same pressure.

While prayer is undeniably an act of religious worship (despite *Marsh*'s approval of it), government-sponsored religious symbols and references present a more complicated issue because they can more easily be seen as a simple "acknowledgement of beliefs widely held among the people of this country" (*Marsh*). Consider, for example, the problem of government celebrations of Christmas. An official Christmas celebration with religious content means that government has singled out Christianity for favorable comment. But to cut the Christian elements out of the displays or ceremonies arguably produces a secularized, historically false version of Christmas; and to eliminate Christmas celebrations altogether prevents government from joining in a popular holiday. Two decisions have struggled with these problems in the context of municipal displays for Christmas and other winter holidays.

In *Lynch v. Donnelly* (S.Ct.1984), the Court upheld the inclusion of a nativity scene, depicting the birth of Jesus, in a city-owned display that also included Santa Claus, reindeer, and other Christmas figures. Following the pattern set the year before in *Marsh*, the Court began by noting the religious references and acknowledgements that have pervaded American government through history: official proclamations of thanksgiving or prayer, official holidays on major religious days, "In God We Trust" on coins, religious paintings in state-run museums. Following *Zorach*, the Court argued that such noncoercive recognitions of religion are necessary to avoid a "callous indifference" to the importance of religion in our culture. "[A] regime of total separation" was neither "possible [n]or desirable," and the *Lemon* test had to be applied in that light.

Examining the display "in the context of the Christmas season," the Court found that its purpose and effect were merely to "take note" of a popular and long-established holiday. It distinguished the creche as an acknowledgement of religion from Bible readings in the public schools (*Schempp*) and the posting of the Ten Commandments in schools as a form of religious "admonition" (*Stone*).

Justice O'Connor, in a concurring opinion, reached the same result but under her own proposed Establishment Clause test: whether the government action, in purpose or effect, communicates a message of "endorsement or disapproval of religion." Such an endorsement "sends a message to nonadherents that they are outsiders, not full members of the political community." Under this standard, government could act in ways that aided religion as long as it sent no message of endorsement. For mostly the same reasons as the majority, she found that the inclusion of the creche in an overall Christmas display sent a message of acknowledging religion rather than endorsing it.

A few years later, however, a fractured Court struck down a Christmas display using Justice O'Connor's "endorsement" test. *Allegheny County v. American Civil Liberties Union* (S.Ct.1989). The county displayed a creche together with a tree and some poinsettias on the main staircase of the courthouse. The city of Pittsburgh, in a nearby city building, erected an 18–foot-high menorah, a branched candle representing the Jewish holiday of Chanukah, next to a 45–foot-high Christmas tree and a sign entitled "Salute to Liberty." The justices struck down the creche display but upheld the menorah display.

The lead opinion by Justice Blackmun gathered a bare majority to judge the case according to the endorsement test, that is, whether government conveyed a message "that religion or a particular religious belief is favored or preferred." The four dissenters, led by Justice Kennedy, argued to limit the Establishment Clause to cases where government coerces citizens to participate in religious activity, and so they voted to uphold both displays. (Changes in the Court's personnel since *Allegheny* have prevented the endorsement test from being adopted in subsequent decisions, but as we saw in *Lee v. Weisman* (see part A–1 above), the Court has not limited the Establishment Clauses to instances of full-fledged coercion either.)

The city's menorah display was approved by the votes of six justices: Blackmun and O'Connor under the endorsement test, and the Kennedy group under the non-coercion test. The crucial swing voters, Blackmun and O'Connor, each argued in separate opinions that the presence of the Christmas tree and the "liberty" sign indicated that the city was sending a message of pluralism, tolerance, and freedom. These two justices differed only on a few details of analysis.

However, the county's creche display was struck down by the votes of five justices—with Blackmun and O'Connor again the swing votes, this time joined by a group of three led by Justice Brennan (these three would have struck down both displays). This majority emphasized that the *Allegheny* creche stood essentially alone; while the creche in *Lynch* stood in the context of many secular symbols, here the other elements such as flowers simply accentuated the religious scene. It did not matter that the Allegheny creche was paid for by a Catholic group; the county could not permissibly endorse the group's religious message any more than it could put forth its own. (This holding must now be read in the light of the *Pinette* decision (see above), which held that religious expression that is truly done by private citizens, and not endorsed by government, is constitutionally protected in the public square.)

Allegheny provides a helpful summary of the subject of religion in government activities—for the various opinions engaged in full battle over whether the Establishment Clause only prevents government from coercing citizens to participate in religious activity. Justice Kennedy, defending the narrower non-coercion test, attacked the broader non-endorsement test on several grounds. As *Marsh* and *Lynch* had shown, American history and traditions are replete with non-coercive religious references by government. To adopt a test disapproving of these, Kennedy argued, would both fly against tradition and signify a "callous indifference" to religion in American life. Moreover, Kennedy said, the endorsement test was too indefinite because it focused on the "minutiae" of each government display to determine whether in context it endorsed religion. Indeed, some observers have scoffed at the case-specific results in *Lynch* and *Allegheny* as creating a a "three plastic reindeer rule" and a "jurisprudence of interior decoration."

In response, the defenders of the no-endorsement approach argued that in a pluralistic society, government should not favor one belief over others, even non-coercively, because such favoritism treats non-adherents as less than full members of the political community. Moreover, to limit the Establishment Clause to cases of coercion would make it a redundancy, since the Free Exercise Clause already prohibits coercion. Even Justice Kennedy admitted that some forms of non-coercive activity by government would go so far as to be an establishment: for example, "the permanent erection of a large Latin cross on the roof of city hall," or to give another example, a simple declaration that "Methodism is the official religion of this state." Kennedy stated that such actions would amount to a subtle form of coercion by "proselytiz[ing]." But as the justices opposing him pointed out, once his standard extended to condemn "proselytizing," it became no more clear than a standard condemning "endorsements." The battle between the non-coercion and non-endorsement camps has not been resolved.

C. DELEGATION OF GOVERNMENTAL POWER TO RELIGIOUS GROUPS

One practice obviously prohibited by the Religion Clauses, particularly the nonestablishment provision, is the actual union of church and state in one institution, exercising both religious and political power, such as the theocracy in Iran. Nothing like that has ever been seen in America, but the Court has struck down laws in two situations that it said contained elements of church-state union. In both cases the government had delegated some of its own discretionary power to be exercised by religious groups.

The Court invalidated a Massachusetts statute that allowed a church or school to veto any application for a liquor license within 500 feet of the church or school. *Larkin v. Grendel's Den* (S.Ct. 1982). Allowing a church to exercise ultimate discretion over liquor applications, a job normally performed by the state liquor commission, produced a "fusion of governmental and religious functions" and thus violated the effect and entanglement prongs of the *Lemon* test.

One difficulty with this holding is that, as Justice Rehnquist's dissent pointed out, state zoning laws can and usually do forbid liquor establishments near churches and schools. So why could the state not exercise the lesser power of leaving the question up to the church? The Court again pointed to the "symbolic union" of giving a church a discretionary government decision. In addition, the church could use its discretion "for explicitly religious goals, for example, favoring liquor licenses for members of that congregation or adherents of that faith."

A more complicated problem was presented in *Board of Education of Kiryas Joel School District v. Grumet* (S.Ct.1994). The Satmar Hasidim, an insular, traditionalist sect of orthodox Jews, lived in their own village in New York state. The state carved out a special school district, drawn along the lines of the village and containing only the Hasidim, to provide publicly-financed special education classes for Satmar children with physical and mental disabilities. The special district was created because the classes could not constitutionally be provided in the Satmar religious schools (see *Aguilar v. Felton*, Chapter 5) and because the children's unusual customs and dress made them very uncomfortable going to classes in local public schools.

The Court held that the creation of the district violated the Establishment Clause. A majority relied on the fact that the state had accommodated the needs of a single religious group without extending the same benefit (a special district) to similarly-situated religious or cultural groups (this holding is discussed in Chapter 3, covering legislative accommodations of religious exercise). But four justices, in an opinion by Justice Souter, also concluded that the state had impermissibly delegated its powers to the Satmar sect. Unlike *Larkin*, the Kiryas Joel statute gave authority to a group of residents, not to a religious institution or leader. But because the residents of the district had been chosen on the basis of their religious affiliation, these four justices saw the result as the same as *Larkin*: the state had purposefully "grant[ed] political control to a religious group."

Conclusion

In reviewing instances of religious activity in government institutions, the Court distinguishes sharply between activity by private citizens and by government. The former is highly protected by the Free Speech and Free Exercise clauses and may not be restricted because of its content or excluded from a forum open to comparable groups, not even to promote a strict separation of church and state. But religious activity by government itself is very likely to be struck down, especially in the public schools. Such activity may violate the Establishment Clause even if it does not explicitly coerce students or other citizens to participate. However, the Court has stopped short of striking down all religious statements by government, especially outside the public schools. This could be because many such practices are traditional, common and familiar, or because they could be seen as merely acknowledging the place of religion in America rather than promoting it.

CHAPTER FIVE

GOVERNMENTAL ASSISTANCE TO RELIGIOUS INSTITUTIONS AND ACTIVITIES

Overview

One of the most important and enduring church-state questions in American history has been whether government may give tax-supported assistance to religious institutions. Most of the modern disputes have involved aid to religiously affiliated schools or social service agencies and whether such aid violates the Establishment Clause. The aid may be in the form of direct monetary payments to the religious institution, payments to persons who attend the religious institution, or the provision of materials or personnel. For many years the modern Court held that many (though not all) forms of aid were unconstitutional. Recent decisions, however, have approved more and more forms of aid provided to religious institutions as part of general programs available to other recipients as well.

A. COMPETING POSITIONS: NO AID AND EQUAL AID

The recurring dispute over government funding has been fought between two positions. One, which might be called the **"no aid"** position, opposes any form of tax-supported aid, or at least any form that could be said to advance the religious mission of the organization.

Proponents of the no aid view rely heavily on the underlying value of church-state separation, in two ways. One set of concerns involves the protection of nonadherents and of society. The provision of aid, it is argued, impermissibly puts government's support behind the particular beliefs of the subsidized organization. Since a religious organization's religious mission often pervades all its activities, government aid is likely to advance that mission—and will assist some faiths more than others. It may also cause dangerous bitterness among religious groups fighting for limited government funds. In addition, opponents argue that the provision of aid violates the religious liberty of taxpayers whose compulsory tax payments are used to provide support to religions with which they disagree. A second separation-based concern is for the autonomy of the religious institution itself: aid is usually accompanied by government regulation (a reason why many religious groups refuse to accept government aid).

The competing position, which may be referred to as **"equal aid,"** argues that religious entities such as schools and social services should be able to receive funding on the same terms as their secular counterparts, public and private. This position relies heavily on the underlying values of equality and religious choice.

Proponents of the equal aid view point out that citizens have the constitutional right, under the Free Exercise Clause and other provisions, to use religious schools or religious agencies. See, e.g., *Pierce v. Society of Sisters* (S.Ct.1925) (striking down law requiring children to attend public schools only). Although these entities teach or promote religion, they also benefit society in other ways by educating children or caring for the needy. Proponents of aid argue that when government pays for such services from its own agencies or from secular private ones, it is a form of discrimination to refuse to pay for the same services from religious schools or agencies just because their programs also teach religion. After all, aid proponents say, the government does not refuse to extend churches other government benefits such as police or fire protection.

In addition, it is argued, a refusal to give equal funding to religious schools or agencies also interferes with citizens' religious choice: they are pressured or encouraged to choose the alternatives to religious schools or agencies, because government subsidizes the alternatives and thus lowers their cost compared to the religious option. To respect free exercise rights, it is asserted, government should be permitted, or perhaps even required, to fund religious schools and agencies as much as it funds their competitors. The provision of such aid, on this view, does not "advance" religion because it does not favor religious over other forms of education.

As was pointed out in Chapter 1, the conflict between the "no aid" and "equal aid" positions was evident in the majority opinion in *Everson v. Board of Education* (S.Ct.1947), the very first modern case on whether governmental assistance violates the Establishment Clause. The Court upheld a public school district's policy of reimbursing parents of parochial school children, along with other parents, for the cost of sending their children to school on local public buses. The majority began with very strong language of church-state separation, stating that "[n]o tax in any amount, large or small, can be levied to support any religious activities or institutions." But it then turned around and approved the payments, citing the free exercise rights of parochial school families and arguing that they should not be denied equal participation in a general program of public benefits. The language of separation gave way to a result based on equal treatment.

Since *Everson*, the Court has decided numerous cases where taxpayers have challenged government funding of religious activities. At first such challenges arose only in state court. In federal court, a person generally does not have standing to challenge the legality of a government spending program simply because he is a taxpayer; for example, I could not object to the legality of the Persian Gulf War just because some of my federal taxes went to pay for it. A federal court plaintiff must be affected by the program in some more distinct and individual way. *Frothingham v. Mellon* (1923).

However, the Court allowed taxpayer challenges to religious aid into federal court in *Flast v. Cohen* (S.Ct.1968). Referring to the history of disputes over aid to religion, *Flast* held that the Establishment Clause was an exception to the general rule against taxpayer standing because it was specifically intended to act as a limitation on the taxing and spending power of Congress. Taxpayer challenges to spending programs may now proceed in either state or federal court. (The Court has refused to extend standing to taxpayers when the provision of aid occurs through something other than spending money, for example by a free grant of government property to a religious institution. *Valley Forge Christian College v. Americans United for Separation of Church and State* (S.Ct.1982). But by far most government aid programs involve the expenditure of tax revenues.)

B. HISTORICAL CONTROVERSIES OVER AID TO RELIGIOUS INSTITUTIONS

Historically, a prime characteristic of official religious establishments was that citizens had to pay taxes to support the official church. This feature of establishments was brought over to the American colonies. By the late 1700s, however, many states had relaxed their policies so that no one denomination received exclusive financial support (see Chapter 2). Today no one seriously suggests that government could compel financial support for one particular church: the modern debate is between "no aid" to any religious institution and "equal aid" to all. That debate has been shaped by two historical controversies and varying interpretations of them.

1. The Virginia Religious Assessment Controversy

The most influential dispute in American church-state history was the fight in Virginia in the 1780s over the tax assessment to support ministers of any denomination. As described in Chapter 2, the assessment was originally designed to be more liberal than earlier taxes levied to support solely the Anglican church. The proposal would have allowed citizens to designate the religious denomination that they wanted to receive their payment. Nevertheless the assessment was defeated after a campaign of opposition led by James Madison together with large numbers of Virginia Baptists and Presbyterians. Madison's "Memorial and Remonstrance Against Religious Assessments" was the most prominent opposition document. Instead of the assessment, Virginia adopted Thomas Jefferson's religious freedom statute, which among other things ended all religious taxes.

Under one leading view, the Virginia episode stands for the "no aid" principle: government may not give direct tax-financed support to religious activity. Moreover, the "no aid" view asserts, this principle was translated into the federal Religion Clauses a few years later. The first modern interpretation of the Establishment Clause, the *Everson* decision, relied heavily on the Virginia controversy, reasoning that "the provisions of the First Amendment, in the drafting and adoption of which Madison and Jefferson played such leading roles, had the same objective and were intended to provide the same protection against governmental intrusion on religious liberty as the Virginia [religious freedom] statute."

From the Virginia episode the *Everson* Court drew the lesson that "[n]o tax in any amount, large or small, can be levied to support any religious activities or institutions, whatever they may be called, or whatever form they may adopt to teach or practice religion." To bolster the argument that aid violates religious liberty, opponents of aid appeal to Jefferson's statement, in the preamble to the religion freedom statute, that "to compel a man to furnish contributions of money for the propagation of opinions which he disbelieves and abhors, is sinful and tyrannical." To bolster the argument that aid threatens the religious institution's own autonomy, opponents point to Madison's statement, in the Memorial and Remonstrance, that establishments have undermined "the purity and efficacy of religion." This interpretation of the Virginia history was most recently set forth in Justice Souter's dissent in *Rosenberger v. Rector of Univ. of Virginia* (S.Ct.1995), which argued that "if the [Establishment] Clause was meant to accomplish nothing else," it was meant to prohibit "[u]sing public funds for the direct subsidization of preaching the word."

Proponents of "equal aid" reply that there are significant differences between the rejected Virginia religious assessment and the modern provision of funds to religious schools or social services. The Virginia tax would have provided funds solely for the activity of preaching religion, when government did not provide tax funds to many comparable activities: by contrast, current proposals for educational or social-service aid allow religiously affiliated agencies that provide such services to receive funds on the same terms as their secular counterparts. This argument was set forth by Justice Thomas in a concurring opinion in *Rosenberger*: "Even if Madison believed that the principle of nonestablishment of religion precluded government financial support for religion *per se* (in the sense of government benefits specifically targeting religion), there is no indication that at the time of the framing he [believed] that the government must discriminate against religious adherents by excluding them from more generally available financial subsidies."

Indeed, Justice Thomas argued, the underlying principles of equality and religious liberty espoused in Madison's Memorial and Remonstrance support the inclusion of religious activities in general government programs, especially today when government subsidizes so many activities. This view is also more consistent, Thomas argued, with other historical instances in which religious institutions have received government benefits.

Still another interpretation, sometimes advanced by proponents of equal aid, is that the Virginia assessment controversy simply is irrelevant to the original meaning of the First Amendment. While Virginia may have adopted a "no aid" position, proponents of this view argue, other states retained tax-supported aid to religion, and the debates surrounding the adoption of the Religion Clauses themselves say nothing to support the no aid position.

The Virginia history continues to be offered as evidence for the position of no direct aid to religion, but as we will see, that position is losing support on the current Court.

2. Protestant–Catholic School Conflicts in the Mid–1800s

The second controversy that has affected how Americans view aid to religious institutions is the conflict in the mid–1800s over the new public schools and the new Catholic school system. Catholic schools sought to obtain government assistance but failed: numerous states explicitly prohibited such funding in their constitutions, even though the attempt to put a bar against funding in the federal Constitution through the Blaine Amendment also was unsuccessful (see Chapter 2).

Opponents of aid use this history not only through the explicit bans in many state constitutions, but also as evidence of a general American tradition forbidding aid to religious schools. As Justice Brennan once argued, "for more than a century, the consensus, enforced by legislatures and courts with substantial consistency, has been that public subsidy of sectarian schools constitutes an impermissible involvement of secular with religious institutions." *Lemon v. Kurtzman* (S.Ct.1971) (Brennan, J., concurring). Although the Court as a whole has not relied explicitly on this tradition, it may be stronger evidence for the "no aid" position than the Virginia dispute is, because it relates directly to educational aid and forbids it even when public schools are subsidized.

In response, however, proponents of equal aid say that the 19th-century bans on aid are irrelevant because they do not reflect the original meaning of the First Amendment and because the attempt to change the federal Constitution through the Blaine Amendment failed. Moreover, they argue, the movement to keep funds from religious schools was "tainted" because it was based on an anti-Catholic animus that is inconsistent with religious liberty and tolerance. The 19th-century opponents of religious school funding fought not for secular schools, but for schools with generic Protestant practices that were unacceptable to Catholics, such as reading the Bible from the King James Version and without interpretation from church authorities. It was partly such practices, and the punishment of Catholic children in the common schools who refused to participate in them, that drove Catholics to set up their own school system. Proponents of equal aid say that the lesson of the mid–1800s is that no school can really be "neutral" between all religious ideas, and thus government can and should provide assistance to schools that operate from a variety of perspectives.

C. THE MODERN CASE LAW: CONFLICTING LINES OF DECISIONS

The Supreme Court's case law concerning government aid is in a stage of evolution, but it does show an overall pattern. As Justice O'Connor remarked in a concurring opinion in *Rosenberger*, *supra*, there are now two well-developed lines of decisions in tension with each other. One line of decisions, largely consistent with the "no aid" position, says that government may not provide funds that can be used for religious purposes. The other line, largely consistent with the "equal aid" position, says that government may provide funds that assist religious agencies as part of a neutral program of benefits that does not create any incentive to choose religious over secular agencies. We will summarize the decisions in each line and then discuss how the Court has resolved or might resolve the two.

1. The "No Religious Uses" Decisions

a. *The Lemon v. Kurtzman Analysis*

The first line of decisions stems from the Court's important ruling in *Lemon v. Kurtzman* (S.Ct.1971). *Lemon* struck down two state programs that gave aid to private elementary and secondary schools, in the form of direct payments to the schools and salary supplements for teachers, for the teaching of secular subjects. As noted earlier (Chapter 1), *Lemon* enunciated and applied a three-part test for Establishment Clause analysis. Under the first part,

the Court said that the aid programs had the valid
"secular purpose" of improving the quality of education in religious schools. (Later decisions have
consistently upheld this purpose for including religious schools in funding programs.) But the aid was
ruled unconstitutional because of a combination of
the last two requirements: a primarily secular effect
and no excessive entanglement between church and
state.

The Court strongly suggested that in order to
avoid having the effect of advancing religion, the aid
must be restricted to teaching in secular subjects—
as indeed the programs in *Lemon* were restricted.
But these restrictions, the Court said, in turn created unconstitutional church-state entanglements.
Keeping religious teaching out of the subsidized
classes would require a "comprehensive, discriminating, and continuing" surveillance because the
schools, nearly all of them Roman Catholic, were
pervaded with religious elements and because
teachers played a central role in maintaining the
religious atmosphere.

Lemon therefore rested explicitly on the combination of two principles of church-state separation:
that government should not give aid to religious
teaching, and that government should not have
significant contact or interaction with religion (the
kind of contact that was required to enforce the
restrictions on the school aid). This combination
created, as the Court later put it, a "Catch 22":
"the very supervision of the aid to assure that it

does not further religion renders the statute inval-id." *Bowen v. Kendrick* (S.Ct.1988).

The premise of *Lemon*—that aid to religious schools could not be of the sort that could be used for religious purposes—became an explicit holding the same day in *Tilton v. Richardson* (S.Ct.1971). The Court held that the government could not give grants to religious colleges to build or repair build-ings without exacting a permanent pledge that the building would not be used for religious purposes; a 20–year restriction was held to be insufficient. Sub-sequently, the Court struck down two forms of aid on the ground that they contained no restrictions and might be used for religious purposes: a program of grants for building maintenance and repair in private elementary schools, and a program of grants and tax credits to parents to reimburse tuition costs at such schools. *Committee for Public Education and Religious Liberty v. Nyquist* (S.Ct.1973).

The Court in these decisions had to explain why giving churches police or fire protection did not similarly aid religion, since any government assis-tance ultimately frees up resources for the institu-tion to use in advancing religion. The Court also had to distinguish two forms of aid upheld in previ-ous rulings: the transportation reimbursements, up-held in *Everson*; and the provision to parochial school students of designated textbooks in secular subjects, upheld in *Board of Education v. Allen* (S.Ct.1968).

One basis for distinction that *Lemon* gave was that safety protection, bus transportation, and secular textbooks could be identified as separate "secular ... or nonideological" aspects of the educational process—unlike aid to teachers, who were heavily involved in teaching religious values, or aid that was unrestricted altogether. This distinction might be questioned with respect to textbooks; but in any event, the distinction reflects the principle that aid is impermissible if it is susceptible to "religious uses." (Another basis for distinguishing *Everson* and *Allen*—that the aid was provided to parents rather than directly to the school—will be discussed in part C–3.)

Another form of church-state "entanglement" also was important in *Lemon* and *Nyquist*. The aid programs had the potential to foster "political division along religious lines," as some religious groups struggled to secure state aid and others opposed it. While political debate and division ordinarily are healthy and to be protected, the Court said, the framers were particularly worried about the hazards of religious conflict in politics. This notion of "political entanglement" reflects one version of the separation value, a version that sees religious disagreements as especially volatile and dangerous to social peace and unity. It therefore seeks to keep politics secular and to keep religion a private matter, not just in the sense that religion is left to nongovernmental entities but in the sense that specifically religious issues should play a limited role in political debate.

The concept of political divisiveness has been criticized on the ground that it discriminates against religious viewpoints and denies the historic influence that religion has had on American politics. (*Lemon* acknowledged this historic role but said the allocation of money was an issue that would intensify division.) In recent decisions, the Court has essentially abandoned the political entanglement doctrine as a reason to strike down aid. See, e.g., *Kendrick, supra* (limiting the notion to aid to religious schools); *Agostini v. Felton* (S.Ct.1997) (holding it an insufficient ground even for invalidating aid to schools).

Still another important premise underlying the "no religious uses" doctrine was set forth in *Nyquist*. The Court said that an aid program including all private elementary schools had the primary effect of advancing religion because nearly all such schools were religiously affiliated. This made the program different from federal student loans or grants for college tuition, which students can use at any college, public or private. But this argument, though it never has been explicitly overruled, may be questioned because it passes over the fact that the government already provides large subsidies to public elementary schools so that they can charge little or no tuition.

Lemon and *Nyquist* also suggested it was troubling that most of the aid to religious schools would flow to one denomination, Roman Catholicism, since few other religious bodies operated such schools. But it could be argued in response that such aid does not favor Catholicism; Catholic schools overall receive more aid simply because there are more of them. (In the years since, the number of Protestant schools has greatly increased, so that Catholics are no longer the only significant recipients of school aid.)

In a series of later decisions, the Court applied the "no religious uses" approach of *Lemon* and *Nyquist* to forbid all but a few forms of aid to religious elementary and secondary schools. A statute paying for the costs of administering and record state-required examinations was struck down on the ground that teacher-administered exams might be influenced by religious doctrine. *Levitt v. Committee for Public Education* (S.Ct.1973). The same reasoning led to the invalidation of laws providing instructional equipment and materials (projectors, recorders, lab equipment, magazines, maps, films and so forth); and the invalidation of laws paying for the cost of transportation on teacher-led field trips. *Meek v. Pittenger* (S.Ct.1975) (equipment and materials); *Wolman v. Walter* (1977) (field trips).

While these decisions left standing the few previous rulings that had approved aid, many observers found the distinctions thin and unconvincing. The Court distinguished the field trips from the transportation reimbursements upheld in *Everson* on the ground that the field trip might include religious instruction. *Wolman*. The difference between allowing the provision of books (*Allen*) and striking down the provision of maps (*Meek*) led one critical senator to ask, only half-jokingly: "What about atlases, which are books of maps?" (The Court continued to say that the textbook case was different because the books had been given to parents, not directly to the school.)

A few limited forms of aid (discussed shortly) survived the *Lemon* approach, but not many. The strictest application of the "no religious uses" approach came in decisions preventing the government from sending public school teachers into religious schools to provide guidance counseling or remedial education in secular subjects. *Meek* banned such a program, and a pair of 1985 decisions reaffirmed this ban and illustrated again the "Catch 22" between the no-effect and no-entanglement rules. (**Note to the reader:** these two decisions have since been overruled (see part C–2 below), but they are discussed here because they still provide a good example of the working of the *Lemon* test.)

In the first decision, *Grand Rapids School District v. Ball* (S.Ct.1985), the Court struck down a local remedial-education program to the extent that it provided classes on the premises of parochial schools. Although most of the justices agreed that paying parochial school teachers to conduct such classes was invalid under *Lemon v. Kurtzman* itself, there was bitter division over whether the same considerations banned the sending of public school teachers into the parochial schools. *Ball* struck down the program by a 5–4 vote on the ground that it did not contain restrictions preventing the teachers from engaging in religious activity.

The companion case, *Aguilar v. Felton,* involved a similar federal program that paid for public school teachers to teach remedial classes to impoverished children in inner-city neighborhoods, but that also imposed restrictions preventing the teachers from teaching religion in the classes. Having struck down the unrestricted local program on the ground of religious effect, the Court struck down the federal program because the restrictions in it created excessive entanglement. The result of these decisions was that remedial classes had to be conducted off the religious school premises—in "neutral" buildings or in mobile vans parked near the schools—which added considerable overhead to the cost of the programs.

The argument for permitting the classes conducted by public school teachers was that they could be trusted not to inculcate religion, since many of them were not members of the denominations operating the religious schools. But the *Ball* majority still found some risk that teachers would "subtly (or overtly) conform their instruction to the [religious] environment in which they teach." The dissents argued that the Court was disregarding the record, which showed no complaints about indoctrination, and allowing even minimal risks to invalidate a worthy program. (The majority responded that the indoctrination might be subtle, or students might be afraid to complain about it.)

The *Ball* majority also advanced two other arguments that, if generally applied, would arguably prohibit any form of aid to religious elementary schools. First, the Court said that placing public school teachers in the religious schools created a "symbolic" connection between church and state and might leave the impression that the government endorsed the school's religious views. Any kind of state aid arguably could be seen in that light. Second, the Court said that the classes "subsidize the religious function of the parochial schools by taking over a substantial portion of their responsibility for teaching secular subjects." But under this logic, does the provision of police or fire protection subsidize religion by freeing the church from having to spend for those protections itself? The Court answered such an argument by noting that the remedial classes went directly to "the educational function" of the school.

The two decisions prohibiting remedial classes conducted by public school teachers were the highwater mark of separationism in the decisions on government aid. However, as will be seen shortly (part C–2), the Court retreated from and eventually overruled these decisions in *Agostini v. Felton* (S.Ct. 1997).

b. *Exceptions: Upholding Aid to Colleges and Social Services Under the Lemon Analysis*

The *Lemon* prohibition on aid that could be used for religious purposes doomed many forms of aid, but not all. At the elementary and secondary school level, the test was extremely strict, but a few limited forms of assistance survived—including, as already noted, transportation reimbursements (*Everson*) and loans of secular textbooks to parents (*Allen*). In addition, the Court upheld subsidies to support speech, hearing, and diagnostic tests for students in religious schools, as long as the tests were objective and allowed no chance for religious discussions or influences to enter. *Wolman v. Walter, supra.* On similar grounds, the Court upheld subsidies to support the giving and scoring of standardized tests, reasoning that such tests would not be religiously influenced, unlike the teacher-prepared tests struck down earlier. *Id.*

(i) Higher education. More important, the Court permitted much more extensive aid to religious colleges and universities. *Tilton v. Richardson* (S.Ct.1971), discussed above, largely approved construction grants to private colleges, including religious ones, for the construction of buildings and facilities used for secular educational purposes. As in *Lemon*, the Court assumed that government funding had to be limited to secular activities in order to be constitutional. But in contrast to *Lemon*, *Tilton* concluded that enforcing such restrictions at the college level would not require continuous or excessive entanglement between church and state.

With respect to religious colleges and universities, *Tilton* said, "there is less likelihood than in primary and secondary schools that religion will permeate the area of secular education." College students are generally "less impressionable and less susceptible to religious indoctrination" than younger students, and many religious colleges "are characterized by a high degree of academic freedom" for both faculty and students. At the four Catholic colleges in question, the Court found that non-Catholics were employed as faculty and admitted as students, students were not required to attend religious services, and even the required theology classes covered many religions and did not seek to proselytize students. The decreased risk of religious elements in the subsidized activities in turn decreased the need for "intensive government surveillance."

As already noted, *Tilton* did find the statutory conditions on the grants to be insufficient in that they only forbade religious uses for subsidized buildings for 20 years. To ensure that government money did not go to advance religion within the meaning of *Lemon*, the Court required that the restriction on religious uses remain as long as the building had any "substantial value." Thus, the Court plainly followed the "no religious uses" approach of *Lemon*, even though it was willing to uphold substantial aid to colleges and universities under this approach.

Subsequently, the Court followed *Tilton*'s reasoning by approving a statute allowing private colleges, including religious ones, to use tax-free bonds from a state government authority to finance the construction of secular facilities. *Hunt v. McNair* (S.Ct. 1973). And it allowed a state to include religious colleges in a program providing "non-categorical" grants that could be used for any purpose that was not "sectarian." *Roemer v. Board of Public Works* (S.Ct.1976).

The Court's distinction between higher education and secondary/elementary education has been criticized as arbitrary: many church-related colleges are in fact permeated with religious elements, while many church-related schools at lower levels are not. Although the U.S. Supreme Court has never confronted such a case, the Virginia Supreme Court refused to allow the use of tax-exempt city construction bonds by Liberty University, headed by the Rev. Jerry Falwell, on the ground that the university was "pervasively sectarian." *Habel v. Industrial Development Authority* (Va.1991). On the other hand, some observers have defended a "bright line" rule distinguishing elementary/secondary from higher education on the basis that it reduces the need for a detailed judicial examination of each school, an inquiry that can itself be intrusive on religious autonomy.

Another objection is that by approving aid to less pervasively religious colleges, the Court has given church-related colleges an incentive to "secularize" their operations in order to receive government funds. See *Roemer* (Stevens, J., dissenting). The tale of Liberty University may be cautionary: after being denied tax-exempt bonds, the university reportedly relaxed a number of its policies, eliminating the requirement that students attend chapel services and allowing faculty more room to take positions at variance with the school's doctrinal beliefs. But what lesson follows from this: that the availability of any funding wrongly tempts a college to compromise its religious standards? Or that colleges should be able to receive aid no matter how religious their atmosphere? The former position would follow the *Lemon* approach even more strictly; the latter approach would reject the premises of *Lemon* and allow substantially more aid.

(ii) Social services. In another important area, the Court has allowed considerable aid to religious social service agencies even under the "no religious uses" approach. Although almost all the modern funding cases have concerned religious schools, religious bodies also operate or sponsor a wide range of health and social services: hospitals, day-care centers, homeless shelters, and so on. Indeed, just as with schools, medical and charitable activities were once primarily the responsibility of religious agencies.

In America it was not until the first half of the 1900s, in the Progressive and New Deal eras, that state and federal government entered these areas on a large scale. An array of government agencies grew up to provide services directly to citizens. But government also worked through private agencies: at the time of a 1981 survey, some 350 federal programs were dispensing more than $46 billion to private social services, about 7 percent of total federal social-service expenditures.

The Court has allowed more substantial aid to these entities than to religious schools, apparently on the ground that medical and social services involve less religious indoctrination than does education, an inherently value-laden and ideological activity. This factor was evident in a turn-of-the-century decision permitting the federal government to pay for the construction of a new building for a Catholic-affiliated hospital in the District of Columbia. *Bradfield v. Roberts* (S.Ct.1899). The Court reasoned that the hospital was not a "religious corporation." It did not confine its medical services to Catholics; it was simply "a secular corporation being managed by people who hold to the doctrines of the Roman Catholic Church, but who nevertheless are managing the corporation according to the law under which it exists."

The *Bradfield* reasoning—that health care services are not distinctively religious even when carried out in a religious setting—explains why the federal government has been able, without constitutional barriers, to give large amounts of money to religious hospitals (among others) under a statute known as the Hill–Burton Act. And indeed, most medical treatments are no different when administered by doctors or nurses of different faiths. There are some exceptions, of course. Catholic hospitals might be ineligible for some forms of funding because they refuse to teach their personnel abortion procedures; and a lower federal court has questioned whether "sanitoriums" applying Christian Science principles of healing are eligible to receive government funds (*Children's Healthcare v. Vladeck* (D.Minn.1996)).

In any event, some social services involve more ideologically charged issues. In 1981, Congress attacked the problem of teenage pregnancy by passing the Adolescent Family Life Act (AFLA), which provided grants to a wide range of government and private agencies, including religious ones, to fund programs for both research into and prevention of teenage pregnancies. The district court struck down the entire statute on the ground that a number of religious agencies had received grants. But the Supreme Court reversed and upheld the statutory program on its face, even though it remanded the case to determine whether grants were unconstitutional in some particular cases. *Bowen v. Kendrick* (S.Ct.1988).

The Court applied the by-now-familiar *Lemon* factors but reached a different result than in school cases. The key difference, the majority said, was that "there is no reason to assume that the religious organizations which may receive grants are 'pervasively sectarian' in the same sense as the Court has held parochial schools to be." Accordingly, again the so-called Catch 22 did not operate: there was no need for the pervasive monitoring of funds that would create entanglement. In contrast to its analysis of schools, the Court was unwilling to assume that most religious social services were permeated with distinctively religious characteristics.

But some of the grantee agencies surely were pervasively religious. Moreover, as Justice Blackmun pointed out in dissent, the particular issue of teenage pregnancy posed a increased likelihood that religious teaching would enter into a program: "There is a very real and important difference between running a soup kitchen or a hospital, and counseling pregnant teenagers on how to make the difficult decisions facing them. The risk of advancing religion at public expense ... is much greater [in the latter case]."

The majority did not dispute these contentions, but instead distinguished between challenges to the statute as a whole ("on its face") and to particular grants under the statute ("as applied"). Although AFLA contained no express provision prohibiting the use of grants for religious teaching, the Court quoted legislative history to the effect that such uses would be improper, and it said that the statute contained sufficient mechanisms for policing against such uses. The fact that some grants would go to "pervasively sectarian" agencies or be used for religious teaching was insufficient to conclude that no religious agencies could receive grants or that the statute should fall as a whole. The Court therefore rejected the facial challenge. But it remanded to the district court to allow the plaintiffs to challenge particular grants if they could prove that the recipient was pervasively sectarian or that it had used it grant for "specifically religious activities."

Kendrick adhered to the *Lemon* test and to the "no religious uses" approach to funding issues. It followed the rule that government funds could not be used in pervasively religious settings or in any activity where religion was taught (the issues that the plaintiffs were allowed to try to prove on remand). The foundations of *Lemon* remained in place, for the time being.

In other respects, however, *Kendrick* pointed to a more hospitable attitude toward direct funding of religiously affiliated institutions (and as such is part of an overall trend in that direction). Most importantly, the Court refused simply to assume that the AFLA grants to religious agencies would inevitably be used for religious teaching. While *Kendrick* itself involved social services, its analysis suggested that the Court might begin to look more carefully at elementary and secondary schools to determine whether in particular instances aid could be limited to "secular" activities of the school. The Court's approach also had a serious practical impact. In *Lemon* and other school cases, plaintiffs had succeeded in using the category of "pervasively sectarian" institutions to achieve quick and inexpensive victories, striking down entire aid statutes on their face, often before they went into effect. By contrast, when *Kendrick* limited the plaintiffs to challenging particular AFLA grants, one by one, it made their case vastly more expensive and time-consuming, perhaps prohibitively so.

In the years since *Kendrick*, policymakers have shown increased interest in delivering social services through religious and other private entities rather than through government agencies. A general dissatisfaction with the performance of government has no doubt contributed to this trend. The 1996 federal welfare reform law includes a provision dubbed "charitable choice," under which welfare recipients can receive vouchers for a variety of services—food pantries, drug and alcohol treatment, day care, job training—and use those vouchers at religiously affiliated agencies, among others. The agencies receiving the vouchers cannot use the money for "sectarian worship, instruction, or prose-lytism," but in other respects they are free to maintain their religious character: keeping religious symbols on the premises, promoting religion in oth-er programs.

If the "charitable choice" provision is challenged, its defenders will surely rely on *Kendrick* to argue that the bar on using the money for worship or instruction satisfies the *Lemon* test and does not create excessive entanglement. But they can also point to another line of decisions holding that gov-ernment does not unconstitutionally advance reli-gion when it provides aid neutrally to individual beneficiaries who can then choose to use it at any agency, public, private, or religious.

2. The "Government Neutrality–Private Choice" Line of Decisions

The second line of decisions on funding has devel-oped in the last fifteen years, after the *Lemon* approach was firmly established, and has allowed much more substantial aid to flow to religious insti-tutions. In these decisions, the Court has approved statutes that provide aid on a neutral basis to beneficiaries who can choose to use it at a wide range of institutions, whether public, secular non-public, or religious. Contrary to the *Lemon* ap-proach, these decisions do not require that religious uses of the aid be forbidden; it is enough that the government treats different uses of the aid equally and the choice of where to use the aid is therefore left to the beneficiary.

This approach first appeared in *Mueller v. Allen* (S.Ct.1983), which upheld a state income tax deduction given to parents for the cost of tuition, books, transportation, and other expenses for their children. Although the Court applied the *Lemon* test, it held that the tax deduction did not have the primary effect of advancing religion because it "neutrally provide[d] state assistance to a broad spectrum of citizens" using public as well as religious and secular private schools. Here, neutrality did not mean no aid to religion, but rather no greater aid to religion than to the alternatives.

The *Mueller* holding might have been limited to tax deductions, where no affirmative assistance was provided by the state. But the Court instead strongly reinforced the emphasis on equality and choice in aid in *Witters v. Washington Department of Services* (S.Ct.1986), holding, unanimously, that the Establishment Clause did not require that state-funded rehabilitation and training classes available to blind students be denied to a man who was studying for the ministry at a Christian bible college.

Witters set forth the foundations of the new approach. Because the state program allowed for aid to be used at a wide range of public and private institutions, any aid "that ultimately flows to religious institutions does so only as a result of the genuinely independent and private choices of aid recipients." Because the statute was neutral as to where the assistance could be used, it "create[d] no financial incentive for students to undertake sectarian education." In short, "the decision to support religious education is made by the individual, not by the State." The aid was analogous, the Court said, to a state employee signing over a paycheck to her church.

The reasoning of these decisions departed dramatically from the premises of *Lemon* and *Nyquist*, as the dissent in *Mueller* pointed out. Those earlier decisions had said that aid to religious schools must be restricted to non-religious uses—"separable secular functions"—in order to be permitted. But there were no such restrictions on the aid in *Mueller* and *Witters*. Tuition deductions defray the cost of the central educational experience, which in a parochial school is often pervaded with religious teaching; and religion could similarly be expected to pervade all activities of the Bible college where Witters received his training.

Under *Lemon*, aid was held to "advance" religion if it was (or even might be) used for religious purposes. But under *Mueller* and *Witters*, government only advances religion if it gives more favorable aid for religious uses or otherwise creates an incentive to choose religious over comparable secular institutions. Neutrality means no greater aid to religion than to alternatives, rather than no aid to religion at all. Thus, under the new decisions, the aid did not have to be restricted to nonreligious uses, and the fact that some beneficiaries would use the aid in religious settings would not make such uses invalid, let alone the overall program. (As a corollary, since the aid did not have to be restricted, no significant surveillance or administrative entanglement was necessary.)

Behind the approval of the relatively minor programs in *Mueller* and *Witters* lies the important, and very politically sensitive, question of whether a state could change its educational system to one of "school choice," under which the state provides equal funding to whatever school a family chooses to send its children. Under the most common proposed format, eligible (usually low-income) families would receive a "voucher" to use at any school they chose. To date, only a few pilot programs have been enacted, mostly in inner-city systems such as Milwaukee and Cleveland.

If a voucher program is enacted, does the inclusion of religious schools in it pass Establishment Clause muster? (If a program excludes religious schools, by far the largest class of private schools, it will have very limited impact.) Under the "no religious uses" reasoning of *Lemon* and *Nyquist*, a voucher system would seem to be invalid because the voucher is not restricted to secular uses. By contrast, the reasoning of *Witters* points in favor of upholding vouchers, which leave the choice of school up to the families and create no incentive to choose religious over other schools.

One argument relevant to the constitutionality of vouchers was previewed in *Witters*. The majority opinion upholding the blind student's training assistance, written by Justice Marshall, found it "important[ ]" that no "significant portion of the aid expended under the Washington program as a whole will end up flowing to religious institutions." Apparently, the fact most of the aid would be used at secular colleges (public and nonpublic) helped show that the "primary effect" of the overall program was not to aid religion. (This fact may explain why the decision was unanimous, attracting even the votes of Justices Marshall, Brennan, and Stevens, who usually opposed aid programs.) If this factor was crucial, then opponents of vouchers arguably could distinguish them from the *Witters* aid on the ground that a significant percentage of vouchers might be used at religious schools.

However, several concurring opinions in *Witters* said that it would not matter what percentage of aid ended up at religious schools. As Justice Powell put it, whatever the percentages, the key was that "the aid was channeled by individual parents and not by the State." *Id.* (Powell, J., concurring). Powell's concurrence was joined by two other justices (Chief Justice Burger and Justice Rehnquist); Justice O'Connor wrote separately endorsing Powell's approach, and Justice White said he "agree[d] with most of Justice Powell's concurring opinion." These five votes in *Witters* may indicate that even if many families chose to use their vouchers at religious schools, the program would still be constitutional because the state's action in providing aid was religiously neutral.

A series of recent decisions have given even greater momentum to the neutrality/choice approach, applying it to approve aid in a wider and wider set of circumstances. In *Zobrest v. Catalina Foothills School District* (S.Ct.1993), the Court held that federal law giving assistance to handicapped students could be applied to pay for a sign language interpreter for a deaf student in a Catholic high school. Again, the key was that the aid could be used at any public or private school and did not create any incentive to attend religious schools. The interpreter might be required to communicate deeply religious messages such as a mass or a theology lecture, as the dissenting opinion pointed out: but it did not matter under the Court's theory, because the religious element was the school's doing and was not in any way changed or magnified by the government employee, who simply communicated whatever words were being said.

The next form of assistance approved was not even to a school that mixed religious teaching with education, but to a publication whose central purpose was to engage in religious witnessing. In *Rosenberger v. Rector of Univ. of Virginia* (S.Ct.1995), the university, a public institution, used an activities fund raised from student fees to provide assistance for a wide range of student publications. However, the university denied assistance to "Wide Awake," a student magazine that analyzed cultural issues from an evangelical Christian perspective, because the university policy had a rule forbidding the funding of religious activities. The Court held not only that including the magazine would be permissible under the Establishment Clause, but indeed that excluding it solely because of its religious content violated the Free Speech Clause. *Id.*; see Chapter 4 (discussing free speech holding).

On the Establishment Clause issue, *Rosenberger* reaffirmed, as a "central" point, that "a significant factor in upholding governmental programs in the face of Establishment Clause attack is their neutrality toward religion." If the magazine received assistance under the university's program, it would receive it not because it was religious, but because it provided "news, opinion, information, opinion, [or] entertainment" as the program guidelines provided. This neutrality distinguished the program from "the levying of taxes upon the public for the sole and exclusive purpose of ... supporting specific sects."

Most recently, the Court pursued the neutrality principle so far as to overrule a separationist decision that had followed the "no religious uses" principle: it reversed itself and upheld the provision of remedial education classes to parochial school students that it had struck down in 1985. *Agostini v. Felton* (S.Ct.1997). The proceeding was reopened at the request of New York City, which sought to free itself from the effects of the earlier rulings (*Grand Rapids v. Ball* and *Aguilar v. Felton*) that had required it to spend millions of extra dollars to hold classes for religious school students off the premises of their schools. The Court granted the relief, holding that more recent decisions "have undermined the assumptions upon which *Ball* and *Aguilar* rested."

The *Agostini* decision continued to apply the test (drawn from *Lemon*) of whether aid had the "effect" of advancing or inhibiting religion; but it remarked that the criteria for assessing the question of effects had changed. Among the major factors the Court mentioned was that the remedial education services "are allocated on the basis of criteria that neither favor nor disfavor religion"—a consideration that *Ball* and *Aguilar* had wrongly given "no weight." Because the program would simply make remedial classes available to all children, it created no incentive to choose religion and was within the line of decisions upholding such neutral aid. (The Court also explicitly rejected two of the bases that *Ball* had given for striking down the programs: the asserted "symbolic link" between church and state from the presence of public school teachers in religious schools, and the fact that the remedial classes freed up resources for the religious schools to pursue religious education.)

However, *Agostini* also made a number of other statements that hedge on the issue of whether government assistance will be approved simply because it is neutral and effectively leaves individuals the choice of where to use it. Similar qualifying language is found in the other recent decisions, *Zobrest* and *Rosenberger*. For now, the Court is proceeding cautiously and leaving open the possibility that some forms of direct monetary aid to religious institutions will still be struck down under the approach of *Lemon* and *Nyquist*.

For example, *Agostini* noted the neutrality of the federal remedial education program but also emphasized that the public school teachers would not be likely to inculcate religion in their classes and should not be presumed to do so. By this reasoning, aid directly to parochial school teachers or their classes might still be invalidated under the theory of *Lemon*: that parochial school teachers, unlike their public school counterparts, are likely to inculcate religion.

In *Rosenberger*, the Court emphasized the neutrality of the university aid program but included a number of qualifications—many of which were also emphasized in a concurring opinion by Justice O'Connor, who provided the crucial fifth vote. One qualification was that the aid came not from a general tax but from a student fee; and Justice O'Connor mentioned the possibility that a student who objected to a certain use of funds might reclaim a pro rata share of the fees she had paid. Perhaps more importantly, the majority opinion emphasized that the aid took the form not of grants to the student magazine, but rather of payments to the third parties that provided the publication services, such as typesetters and printers. The majority noted previous decisions that had "recognized special Establishment Clause dangers where the government makes direct money payments to sectarian institutions" (citing decisions from the *Lemon* line), and it did not quarrel with that principle but simply said it was inapplicable because the university's payments went to third parties.

Zobrest, likewise, followed the neutrality/choice approach but also noted that with the provision of a sign language interpreter, "no funds traceable to the government ever find their way into sectarian schools' coffers." The qualifying language in these two decisions arguably leaves room for the Court to invalidate "direct money payments" to religious schools—or even vouchers channeled through parents, since under a voucher system money stemming from government does ultimately go into religious school coffers.

However, for the Court to invalidate a voucher program (or even a program of direct money grants) that was neutral and created no incentive for religious schooling would seem to conflict with the principles of equality and choice, which by now are solidly established by a series of decisions. The Court's current doctrine is thus still in a state of internal conflict. It is worth taking a moment, then, to ask to more pointedly whether the two lines of decisions can be reconciled.

3. Resolving the Two Lines of Decisions

How, if at all, will the Court resolve the difference between the *Lemon/Nyquist* line of decisions prohibiting any religious uses of funds, and the *Mueller/Witters/Zobrest* line permitting funds to go to religious schools on a neutral basis? Some bases for distinction fail to explain the decisions. Under the "neutrality-choice" line, the Court has approved not only tax benefits but also affirmative forms of aid to families using religious schools. It also has approved such aid not only at the college level but at the elementary and secondary levels as well.

One distinction that accounts for many of the decisions is between aid given directly to religious institutions and aid given to individuals and families who then may use it at a religious institutions. Direct aid was struck down in the *Lemon/Nyquist* line of decisions, indirect aid upheld in many of the *Mueller/Witters* decisions. The distinction could be defended on the ground that indirect aid achieves a greater symbolic separation between church and state by interposing the action of a private citizen. Moreover, passing aid through citizens ensures that it arrives at a religious institution only as a result of "genuinely individual and private choices" (*Witters*). By contrast, direct aid requires the state to decide how much funding religious institutions shall receive, which can create political controversy and can produce allocations that do not reflect the choices of citizens about using religious versus other agencies.

However, the direct/indirect distinction has problems as well. Direct aid can similarly avoid distorting citizens' choice if each school or agency simply receives an allocation according to the number of students or beneficiaries who have chosen to go there for services. Moreover, the categories of direct and indirect aid shade into each other. *Zobrest*, for example, distinguished the permissible provision of a sign-language interpreter from "direct grants" of government aid prohibited (at that time) under *Grand Rapids v. Ball*: but what is the difference between providing a sign-language interpreter and providing remedial-education teachers? The Court's approval of the latter in *Agostini v. Felton* further undercuts the direct/indirect distinction.

The suggestion that the particular constitutional wrong is for cash to end up in a religious institution's coffers (*Zobrest, Rosenberger*) can explain many of the decisions, but it could be criticized on the ground that is has little basis in economic reality. Aid in forms other than cash grants—provision of personnel, payment to third-party vendors—has been approved although gives just as much assistance to the religious institution as do cash grants.

Another possible distinction between programs might rely on the Court's reasoning in *Nyquist* that an aid program cannot be limited to private schools because nearly all of those are religious: only an aid program that encompasses public as well as private schools can be approved. This reasoning has recently been used to challenge experimental voucher programs that provide vouchers for use at any private school. And the Court itself relied on the distinction in *Mueller v. Allen* to uphold the tax deduction that on its face was available to parents of public school children as well as others. But as was discussed above (part C–1), the distinction seems to overlook the fact that government already gives aid to public schools; a specific program aiding private schools can be seen simply as an effort to include them in the overall mix of funding.

The Court may well opt for a distinction that preserves both the *Lemon/Nyquist* decisions and the *Mueller/Witters* decisions. But any such distinction seems likely to be imperfect, for the premises of the two lines of decisions are in tension.

D. STATE CONSTITUTIONAL PROHIBITIONS ON RELIGIOUS AID

However, even if neutral state aid to religious schools is permitted under the Establishment Clause, it still faces a barrier in many states from state constitutional provisions that are far more explicit and strict in prohibiting aid to religious schools. These provisions reflect more clearly the value of separation, seeking to avoid the kind of church-state interaction that aid programs bring about. As discussed above (part B–2), many such provisions were passed in the 19th century to ensure that state funds went only to public schools and not to Catholic schools. More than twenty state constitutions expressly prohibit government from appropriating money or property to aid a religious sect; many of the same states, as well as some others, have provisions specifically prohibiting state aid for sectarian schools.

The operation of the stricter state constitutional provisions is exemplified by the subsequent history of the *Witters* case. After the U.S. Supreme Court ruled that giving rehabilitation assistance to Witters at his bible college would not violate the Establishment Clause, the case was remanded to the Washington Supreme Court. That court held that, notwithstanding the federal ruling, extending aid to Witters would violate the state constitutional provision that "no public money or property shall be appropriated for or applied to any religious worship, exercise or instruction, or the support of any religious establishment." *Witters v. State Commission for the Blind* (Wash.1989).

Under the Washington provision, the court held, it was enough that aid in the particular case was being used to support a religiously oriented education. It did not matter that the aid statute was neutral and left this decision up to the beneficiary (the factors that had been crucial to the U.S. Supreme Court). This result followed from the text of the state provision, which said that public money not only could not be "appropriated for" religious instruction, but could not be "applied to" it either. The provision, which was adopted as part of the 19th century wave of bans on funding, was "sweeping and comprehensive," the court said, and broader than the federal rule. See also *Jackson v. Benson* (Wis.App.1997) (relying on similar provision in Wisconsin constitution to strike down inclusion of religious schools in voucher program for Milwaukee-area schools).

Because state constitutional bans on funding of religious activities are so common, the increasing approval of funding by the U.S. Supreme Court may have limited effect in many states. However, a state constitutional ban might be overridden in two ways. First, if the statute providing aid is a federal one, it will override a state constitutional ban because of the Supremacy Clause of Article VI, section 2 (federal laws are the "supreme law of the land, ... any thing in the constitution or laws of any state to the contrary notwithstanding").

Second, if the inclusion of religious entities in neutral aid programs is not just permitted by the First Amendment, but actually required by it, states could not deny such aid in a discriminatory fashion. Under the Supremacy Clause of Article VI, § 2 of the Constitution, the federal constitutional right would override any state constitutional rule. See also *Widmar v. Vincent* (S.Ct.1981) (exclusion of religious group from open state university forum could not be justified by state constitutional interest in strict separation of church and state). To this question we now turn.

E. THE IMPLICATIONS OF FREE EXERCISE AND FREE SPEECH

Some proponents of the equal aid view have argued not just that the government is constitutionally permitted to include religious institutions in an overall funding program on the same terms as other institutions, but that it is constitutionally required to include them. These equal aid proponents argue that not funding religious institutions when other institutions are funded is a form of discrimination that violates both the Free Exercise and Free Speech clauses. On the free speech issue, these challengers rely on the holding of *Rosenberger* that denying funding to a student publication because it was religious was a form of forbidden viewpoint discrimination (see part C–2). On the free exercise issue, the challengers point to the rule of *Lukumi v. City of Hialeah* (S.Ct.1993) and *Employment Division v. Smith* (S.Ct.1990) that government is forbidden to single out religion for discriminatory treatment (see Chapter 3).

The Court rejected this argument a number of years ago without explanation in a summary decision, which suggests that it saw no merit whatsoever in the claim. *Luetkemeyer v. Kaufmann* (S.Ct. 1974). And even if the current Court continues to permit equal aid to religious institutions, it is questionable whether it would go so far as to require that the aid be equal. As noted above (part C–2), *Rosenberger* was carefully limited to leave open the question whether the equal treatment principle would encompass monetary payments to religious institutions. And the Court might likewise conclude that the free exercise rule of nondiscrimination set forth in *Smith* does not apply to the situation of affirmative money payments to religious institutions.

Conclusion

For many years, the Court followed the approach that government aid could not be extended to religious organizations if some of that aid could be used for the organization's religious purposes. Under this approach, the Court struck down most forms of aid to religious elementary and secondary schools; but it allowed considerable aid to religious colleges and social services on the ground that religion did not pervade all their activities, so the subsidized functions could be separated from religion. This approach, which was based in the value of church-state separation but did not follow it in all circumstances, produced results that many criticized as internally inconsistent, and some criticized as unfair to religious education.

Recently, the Court has followed a different approach that allows aid to to religious organizations, even aid that would support their religious purposes, as long as the terms of the statute are equal for all recipients and create no incentive to practice religion. This approach rests more on values of equality and religious choice. But although the Court has repeatedly applied this new approach, it has never fully repudiated the old one. Some distinctions have been suggested to reconcile the two lines of decisions; but they coexist uneasily, and sooner or later the Court is likely to have to resolve them.

CHAPTER SIX

RELIGIOUS INFLUENCES ON POLITICAL DECISION– MAKING

Overview

To this point, our discussion of church-state issues has focused on situations in which the government directly promotes or restricts religious activity. Questions concerning explicit state-sponsored religious symbols or exercises, governmental aid to religious institutions, and prohibitions or restrictions on religious exercise make up the vast majority of the Supreme Court's case law on religion and the state. But religion and government interact in an even more pervasive way: through the countless issues of justice, morality, and social good that are the subject matter of political debate and legislation.

Most religious faiths, especially those in the Jewish and Christian traditions, claim to set forth standards of social justice and morality, and therefore they make assertions about what sorts of laws should be enacted. To what extent should or may government, in passing laws on matters within its jurisdiction—the economy, criminal justice, civil rights—act on the basis of religious doctrines, standards, or values? That is the subject of this chapter.

Historically, as we will see, American politics and law have constantly been influenced by religious doctrines and values, and many observers argue that this is perfectly normal and proper in a democracy so many of whose citizens are religious. But other observers argue that in a pluralistic society, there must be limits on government's reliance on religious grounds. They argue that many religious doctrines are not widely shared throughout the population, and thus for government to enforce laws based on such doctrines is to impose religious conformity on the population, as surely as if the government forced people to pray particular prayers. Critics of religious involvement also express concern for the purity of religion, warning that political involvement tends to distract religious bodies from their primary spiritual mission.

Arguments against heavy religious involvement in politics thus sound both typical themes of church-state separation: the protection of society and especially non-adherents from government-imposed religion, and the protection of religion from corruption by its association with government.

The subject of religion in political decision-making is one on which First Amendment case law has been relatively unimportant; while the Supreme Court has decided very few cases on the subject, political and legal theorists have carried on a lively discussion about the extent to which laws should be based on religious grounds. Many of the arguments advanced in the previous paragraph have been presented not as matters of constitutional law, but as matter of prudence and political morality: not how the government is legally required to behave, but how a good citizen or legislator should behave act in a free society.

This is also a subject of great importance and sensitivity to many people. Without going too far on a limb, it seems likely that much recent concern about the political activity of conservative religious bodies stems from a fear not that everyone will be forced to practice conservative religion, but that everyone will be forced to obey laws reflecting conservative religious values (particularly in areas of sexual morality such as abortion and homosexuality).

A. HISTORY: THE INVOLVEMENT OF RELIGION IN AMERICAN POLITICS

The Puritans who settled Massachusetts in the 1600s expressly wished, in the words of their leader John Winthrop, expressly to build a "city on a hill" in which society would be governed by Christian principles. They were theological heirs to John Calvin, deeply convinced that the sovereignty of God must be expressed over all aspects of life. Ever since then, religious beliefs have been a potent force in American politics and law—sometimes for good, sometimes for ill—even in the much more secular and religiously diverse atmosphere of today. Religious bodies have sometimes had qualms about being distracted from spiritual matters by politics, but such reservations have never stopped them when they believed the cause to be sufficiently important.

Agitation for the American Revolution came in significant part from evangelical preachers fueled by the Great Awakening of the mid–1700s. In the 1800s, religious revivals spun off into political movements advocating reforms such as the abolition of slavery, the prohibition of liquor sales and gambling, and the granting of suffrage to women. Arguments from the Christian scriptures figured prominently on both sides of the slavery debate: abolitionists claimed that slaves were men and women created in God's image, while slavery apologists answered that God had ordained that Negroes were inferior. Protestant nativists sought to restrict the (mostly Roman Catholic) immigration of the mid–1800s on the ground that the authoritarian structure of the Catholic Church had not prepared the newcomers to respect or exercise the values of democracy.

In the early 1900s, some religious bodies joined the fight for legal regulation of industry, espousing the "Social Gospel" doctrine that the Kingdom of God should be translated into decent wages and working conditions. Others followed the individualistic tendencies of Protestantism and supported a laissez-faire system. The movements for liquor prohibition and women's suffrage finally succeeded in

amending the Constitution (the former only briefly).

Fundamentalist Protestants lost their battle in
the 1920s to ban the teaching of evolution in public
schools, and then largely retreated to work on
building up their own churches, schools, and other
institutions. For some time, they sounded the
theme that mixing religion and politics was bad for
religion because it distracted it from its task of
"saving souls." But other churches became more
consistently active in politics. The movement to
repeal segregation and enact civil rights laws was
led in large part by black ministers, from Martin
Luther King down through hundreds of local activ-
ists. Scripture references and the lyrics of hymns
and spirituals pervaded King's famous speeches as
well as most other aspects of civil rights rallies.
Liberal white churches eventually joined the movement, culminating in a broad effort to enact the
Civil Rights Act of 1964, which one of its sponsors,
Senator Hubert Humphrey, said would never have
passed without church support. Many religious bodies now maintain full-time lobbying offices in Washington and some state capitals.

Conservative Protestants emerged from their political insularity in the 1970s, seeking to enact laws
restricting abortion and homosexuality, restoring
school prayer, assisting the nation of Israel, and
reducing government regulation and taxes. It
seemed ironic that groups who had condemned the
mixing of religion and politics (especially during the
civil rights era) now mobilized voters and lobbied

for legislation. But it also seemed ironic that some liberals condemned the Religious Right for mixing religion and politics, given the central role of religion to causes such as civil rights.

B. CONSTITUTIONAL CASE LAW

For years, one prong of the test of *Lemon v. Kurtzman* (S.Ct.1971)—the requirement that legislation must have a "secular purpose"—suggested that a law might face Establishment Clause difficulties simply because it was based on religious tenets. If a law lacked a secular purpose, that was enough to invalidate it regardless of its effect. From the 1960s through the mid–1980s, the Court did strike down a number of laws on the ground of no secular purpose. And in at least three such decisions, the Court pointed to the religious motivations of legislators who had been active in passing the laws.

In striking down Louisiana's statute mandating "balanced treatment" of creationism and evolution, the Court noted that the statute's legislative sponsor had been motivated by the fact that evolution contradicted his religious tenets of Biblical literalism. *Edwards v. Aguillard* (S.Ct.1987). Earlier, in striking down Arkansas' law prohibiting the teaching of evolution, the Court pointedly noted that "[i]t is clear that fundamentalist sectarian conviction was and is the law's reason for existence" *Epperson v. Arkansas* (S.Ct.1968). And in striking down Alabama's law mandating a moment of silence "for meditation or voluntary prayer," the

Court noted that the sponsor had stated his goal in adding the words " ... or voluntary prayer" was " 'to return voluntary prayer' to the public schools." *Wallace v. Jaffree* (S.Ct.1985). Other decisions finding a non-secular purpose include *Stone v. Graham* (S.Ct.1980) (posting of Ten Commandments on classroom wall); *Abington School Dist. v. Schempp* (S.Ct.1963) (official Bible readings in schools); and *Engel v. Vitale* (S.Ct.1962) (officially composed prayers in schools).

However, these decisions have not come to stand for the broad principle that a religious motivation for a law is enough to make the law unconstitutional. The Court has emphasized that only if a law has no significant secular purpose whatsoever does it flunk the first part of the *Lemon* test—even if legislators may also be intending to help religion. For example, as noted in Chapter 5, the Court has uniformly ruled that programs providing funds to religiously affiliated schools serve the secular purpose of improving educational quality in those schools.

To hold broadly that laws may not be based on religious reasons or arguments would create tension with the Court's holdings that religious groups and individuals are entitled to full rights of political speech and activity. See, e.g., *McDaniel v. Paty* (S.Ct.1978) (striking down law barring ministers from serving in state legislature); see also *Rosenberger v. Rector of University of Virginia* (S.Ct.1995); *Lamb's Chapel v. Center Moriches School District* (S.Ct.1993) (both holding that religious viewpoints may not be excluded from forum open to other viewpoints on the same topic). The Court has recognized that "[a]dherents of particular faiths and individual churches frequently take strong positions on public issues.... Of courses, churches as much as secular bodies and private citizens have that right." *Walz v. Tax Commission* (S.Ct.1970). If the presence of religious activity behind the passage of a law counted against its constitutionality, those who support the law for religious reasons might well be "chilled" from expressing their viewpoint in the debate over the law.

It is notable, then, that all of the decisions finding no secular purpose involved the sensitive context of public schools, and that nearly all of them involved explicitly religious exercises, symbols, or teachings. Arguably, when the government explicitly singles out religion for promotion and indoctrination, it cannot be intending any broad secular purpose to which the advancement of religion is simply incidental. Most of these decisions, however, could also be explained simply on the ground that the laws in question explicitly promoted the government's preferred form of religion. (The law in *Epperson*, which merely prohibited the teaching of evolution, fits within this category less easily; but the decision could be defended on the ground of the free speech and academic freedom rights of school teachers.)

Outside of the public schools context, in the areas of social or economic policy, challengers have had much less success in objecting to religious influences on legislation. In *Harris v. McRae* (S.Ct.

1980), the Court unanimously rejected a claim that the Hyde Amendment, which denies federal Medicaid funds for most abortions, violated the Establishment Clause "because it incorporate[d] into law the doctrines of the Roman Catholic Church concerning the sinfulness of abortion." The Court said that a law does not violate the Establishment Clause just because it "happens to coincide or harmonize" with a religious tenet. The anti-abortion law was "as much a reflection of 'traditionalist' values towards abortion, as it [wa]s an embodiment of the views of any particular religion."

Interestingly, in *Harris* the National Council of Churches, a strong opponent of restrictions on the right to abortion, filed a "friend of the court" brief arguing that the religious influences on the Hyde Amendment should not render it unconstitutional. The Council's position most likely reflected the fact that religious groups such as it speak out and try to influence government on a wide range of legislation with moral implications.

Similar reasoning to that in *Harris* underlay the Court's earlier decision rejecting an Establishment Clause challenge to state laws that prohibited many forms of business activity on Sundays. *McGowan v. Maryland* (S.Ct.1961). The challengers had argued that Sunday closing laws were designed simply to enforce the observance of the Christian sabbath. The Court answered, over the lone dissent of Justice Douglas, that although the laws originally had that religious purpose, they had come to rest on secular grounds: promoting a common day of relaxation for all citizens, on the day of the week that most people would select of their own accord. As with the Hyde Amendment, Sunday laws simply coincided with the tenets of religious believers. The laws' few lingering references to "the Lord's Day" did not overcome the secular purpose.

Although *Harris* and *McGowan* both upheld religiously influenced laws, the decisions do leave open the possibility that a facially secular law in the social or economic sphere could entirely lack a secular purpose and thus be unconstitutional. Justice Stevens made such an argument concerning a state abortion statute in his dissent in *Webster v. Reproductive Health Services* (S.Ct.1989), where the Court rejected challenges to various provisions of a Missouri law limiting abortions. The statute's preamble declared the legislature's belief that "life begins at conception." The majority dismissed the challenge to the preamble on the ground that it did not actually restrict the challengers' activities in any way. But Stevens would have invalidated the preamble on the ground that it lacked any secular purpose and merely stated the Catholic Church's theological position on abortion. "Bolstering" his conclusion, he said, was the fact the "intensely divisive character" of the abortion debate reflects the religious convictions of both sides, and the government may not "foment such [religious] disagreement."

It seems unlikely, however, that a majority of the Court will strike down many laws on the ground that they lack any secular purpose. Consider, for example, *Bowers v. Hardwick* (S.Ct.1986), where the Court rejected a claim that laws against sodomy infringed on the constitutional right to privacy implicit in the Due Process Clause. Justice Blackmun, dissenting, suggested that the laws could not be based on anything other than "conformity to religious doctrine"; but the majority ignored his argument and noted that sodomy laws "have ancient roots." If the fact that a certain rule has traditionally been enforced is a permissible government purpose, then many religiously based laws could be shielded from Establishment Clause attack, since religious doctrines provided the historical impetus for many of our most long-standing laws.

That is not to say, of course, that religiously motivated laws might not be invalidated on other constitutional grounds. For example, in *Romer v. Evans* (S.Ct.1996), the Court held that a state constitutional prohibition on any gay rights laws, ordinances, or policies by state or local agencies within the state was based on an "irrational" animus toward homosexuals as a class and thus violated the Equal Protection Clause. But the Court did not refer to the fact that the measure was fueled largely by conservative religious activity. Instead, it said that the measure was so broad and so unnecessary that its provisions could only be explained by simple animus toward homosexuals.

In a somewhat different vein, in *Planned Parenthood v. Casey* (S.Ct.1992), the Court largely reaffirmed the right to abortion declared in *Roe v. Wade* (S.Ct.1973). The crucial opinion, authored by three key justices, relied heavily on the fact that *Roe* should be deferred to as a matter of precedent. But it also defended the right to individual decisionmaking in abortion and other "intimate and personal matters" on the ground that "[a]t the heart of liberty is the right to define one's own concept of existence, of meaning, of the universe, and of the mystery of human life. Beliefs about these matters could not define the attributes of personhood were they formed under the compulsion of the state."

Both of these decisions could be read to impose constitutional limits on the state's enacting laws because of religious convictions about the sinfulness of the behavior being prohibited. Some conservative critics charged that the *Romer* Court was implicitly holding that traditionalist religious beliefs about homosexuality are irrational. And the passage in *Casey* could be read to forbid legislation touching on questions about the "meaning" or "mystery of human life"—that is, questions to which religious views have historically spoken. But nevertheless, both of these decisions rested on other constitutional doctrines besides the Religion Clauses (equal protection and substantive due process), and neither relied specifically on the fact that the laws in question were religiously motivated. (Indeed, the broad language in *Casey* about the "mystery of human life" was significantly scaled back in *Washington v. Glucksberg* (S.Ct.1997), where the majority refused to extend the right to liberty in intimate matters to encompass a right to physician-assisted suicide. The majority said that the *Casey* passage was merely a description of those areas of life that had historically been recognized as matters of individual privacy.)

In addition to the history of religious involvement in politics, there is another reason why courts arguably should be reluctant to strike down a law solely because of its religious motivation: the problem of determining a legislature's motive. Different lawmakers may have voted for a law for a number of reasons, even reasons unrelated to its merits (such as returning a favor to a legislative colleague). It will often be difficult to attribute one actual motive to the entire body. In addition, among the legislators' purposes will almost always be some secular ones; one can rarely say that a law is based solely on religious motivations. Indeed, someone who believes a certain position is commanded by God is also quite likely to believe that it is good for human beings in secular terms as well.

With the decline of the *Lemon* test, challenges based solely on the religious motivation of a law seem even less likely to succeed than before. The position that laws should not be based on religious motivations rests on the premises of church-state separationism: that because religious differences are both intensely divisive and not necessary to the resolution of social questions, government should confine itself to secular reasons for acting. The arguments for permitting laws to be based on religious motivations appeal to notions of equal treatment; they claim that religious views should be considered in the political arena just like any other views. As the Court's primary goal in church-state disputes shifts away from maintaining separation and toward maintaining equality between religion and non-religion, the case for striking down laws because of their religious motivations seems less likely to appeal to the justices.

C. PHILOSOPHY: RELIGION AND POLITICS IN A PLURALISTIC LIBERAL DEMOCRACY

While the Court appears to have cut off most constitutional attacks on the religious motivation behind laws (except in the context of public schools), a vigorous debate on the issue continues among legal theorists and in the broader culture. Even if lawmakers and citizens are free as a matter of constitutional law to act based on religious motivations and arguments, there is a separate question whether it is ethical or prudential for them to do so. As Professor Kent Greenawalt, a leading thinker on the subject, has put the question: "What grounds are proper for people making political decisions and arguments within a liberal democracy?" *Private Consciences and Public Reasons* (1995).

At one end of the spectrum, some theorists argue that it is generally illegitimate, as a matter of political morality even if not of constitutional law, for citizens or officials to rely on religious grounds in arguing for or enacting laws. Proponents of this "no reliance" view claim that in a liberal society with a variety of religious beliefs, no one should rely on or publicly present a ground for lawmaking that is not widely shared by other citizens or that rests on some claim of a "privileged" access to truth, such as divine revelation, that is not open to all. The "widely shared" grounds for acting that these theorists endorse include empirical investigation (both in the natural sciences and the social sciences), logical reasoning and inquiry, and some moral affirmations that are basic to the constitutional order, such as the equal dignity of all human beings and the importance of democracy.

Logically, this restriction on making arguments that are not widely shared would extend to moral and philosophical views that are not religious in the sense of dealing with ultimate questions or the nature of God, but that are still "inaccessible" to many citizens because they cannot be verified empirically or established logically or are not among the basic rules of our constitutional system. For example, the ethical philosophy of Kant is not widely shared among the general population, and it is highly debatable whether its affirmations can be proven either empirically or logically.

However, some proponents of the no reliance view have been particularly concerned with the dangers of religious grounds in politics, over and above any problems posed by other ideologies. They argue that religious positions are especially difficult to verify, or even to argue about rationally, and thus have a special tendency to create divisiveness and even violence when they are injected into the political sphere.

At the other end of the debate, some theorists argue that citizens and legislators are morally free to rely on their religious beliefs in acting and arguing as fully as they would any other beliefs. The proponents of this "full reliance" view say that to limit the role of religious values in politics is inconsistent with American history, conflicts with democracy because so many Americans are religious, and unfairly disfavors religious views and the citizens and legislators who hold them.

The proponents and opponents of religious participation in lawmaking disagree on several important questions. Perhaps most importantly, those who oppose religious grounds for lawmaking proceed from the premise that government can be "neutral" toward religion by relying neither on religious nor explicitly anti-religious premises. Government, in this view, should use the "common denominator" of widely shared secular reasons. By contrast, those who take the full-reliance position argue that excluding religious grounds is not neutral but distorts the debate in favor of views that treat religion as unimportant or as not morally binding. For many religious people, there is no common denominator; they may agree with certain secular views, but only on religious grounds from which they cannot separate themselves.

The two positions also tend to have some differences about the nature of political decisionmaking. Some proponents of the no-reliance view emphasize that the goal of politics in a democracy is to promote deliberation among all citizens about the common good, and thus only those grounds that all citizens can in principle accept—that is, that are widely shared—are appropriate premises for political discussion. The full-reliance position tends to rest more on the notion that all citizens come to the political table with certain views, which are not likely to be changed in political debate, and therefore all views should be counted and the majority prevail.

In addition, however, the two positions also disagree about what moral values or grounds are widely shared and acceptable. Those committed to the no-reliance view argue that religious appeals inherently exclude those citizens outside that particular religious tradition. But defenders of full reliance argue that among American citizens as a whole, no set of symbols and concepts is more widely known and shared than those of the Jewish and Christian traditions—far more widely shared than many of the philosophical views, such as utilitarianism or Kantianism, that theorists commonly employ to discuss legal questions.

The two positions also disagree on what conclusions to draw from the history of religious involvement in politics in America and elsewhere. The supporters of full reliance argue that limiting the role of religious values in politics is out of keeping with American traditions and will deprive politics of the kind of moral fervor that fueled movements like those for abolition and civil rights. While the supporters of full reliance admit that religious arguments have also produced injustice, they say they we cannot have the good without the bad. They point out that in the 20th century, secular ideologies such as Nazism and Communism (both of which were hostile to traditional religion) have caused far more widespread conflict and suffering than any religious disputes have.

The no-reliance supporters respond that valuable laws such as anti-slavery and civil rights laws could be fully justified on secular grounds; that the same pervasive public religiousness in American history has also produced bigotry against religious minorities like Catholics, Jews, Mormons, and Jehovah's Witnesses; and that in today's even more pluralistic religious conditions, government reliance on any one set of doctrines is bound to exclude more and more citizens.

Finally, the two positions disagree on whether it is practically necessary to have a moral restriction on explicit religious arguments in politics. Supporters of full reliance argue that the very fact of pluralism means that narrow religious arguments are likely to be unsuccessful because they will not appeal to many citizens. For example, if a legislator presses to make certain conduct illegal just because the Bible says it is sinful, he is not likely to convince anyone who does not accept the Bible as the only or last word on moral questions. That may be true nationally, supporters of the no-reliance position answer, but in particular localities very specific religious doctrines may command a majority and be used to restrict the conduct of those who do not adhere to the doctrines.

Some theorists have attempted to carve out intermediate positions on the question of religious grounds in politics. A number of writers have suggested that religious arguments may carry moral weight in politics but only if they are "ecumenical" or "non-sectarian" in nature, that is, if they appeal to reason or broadly shared values and not to non-shared sources of authority such as the statements of a scripture or a religious leader. This position, which was once taken by Professor Michael Perry in a book entitled *Love and Power* (1991), shares some features with the no-reliance position. Both say that only publicly accessible or shared grounds of decisionmaking should be considered; the difference is that Perry argued, quite vigorously, that many religious arguments in America are publicly accessible to most citizens and amenable to reason. (In that regard he agreed more with the full-reliance position.) Such "ecumenical" arguments could be based on familiar religious concepts such as the equality of all humans before God, or stories such as that of the Good Samaritan who cared for his injured neighbor. Therefore, Perry claimed, such arguments are morally acceptable.

The position favoring "ecumenical" or "reasoned" religious beliefs seeks to reap the perceived benefits of religious discourse in politics, while avoiding the perceived dangers of narrow or dogmatic views that make no effort to engage in dialogue with or learn from other groups. But not surprisingly, Professor Perry's position received sharp criticism from those who believe that no view should be dismissed from public debate by labelling it "sectarian" or "non-accessible." Perry's position rested in part on a claim about what kind of religious faith is most authentic: faith that sees its beliefs as fallible and open to revision through learning from others. Critics such as Professor David Smolin argued that Perry was simply trying to impose his own ideals of good religion as restrictions on public debate. (Perry himself has since modified his views to allow all religious views into public moral debate.)

Another intermediate position is advanced by Professor Kent Greenawalt, who argues that officials and citizens may legitimately rely on religious grounds in reaching decisions (whom to vote for, what laws to support), but that they generally should make public arguments only on widely shared, publicly accessible grounds. *Private Consciences and Public Reasons*, *supra*. Greenawalt generally emphasizes the drawbacks of widespread religious references in public political debate. But he argues that religion can be a legitimate basis for a citizen or legislator's actual decision (as opposed to her public arguments), because it is too difficult for people to separate their religious beliefs from the other grounds that influence them, and because other grounds will often be insufficient to give a clear answer on debated political issues.

Greenawalt's approach has received criticism because it drives a wedge between people's actual decisions (where he says religious grounds are morally legitimate) and their public arguments (where he says religious grounds should be omitted). The result, critics say, is dishonesty in public debate and an inability to learn and understand each other's real views.

Greenawalt replies that it is common for people to defend actions on more limited grounds than what actually motivated the action: lawyers, for example, regularly make arguments for their clients on only those grounds that are likely to be most persuasive to a court. Once people understand the limited role of public debate, Greenawalt says, they will not think it is hypocritical to refrain from publicly stating every ground for their decisions.

Greenawalt makes one important exception to his thesis that officials may rely on religious values in making decisions. Judges, he says, should strive to follow publicly accessible secular reasons not only in justifying their rulings publicly, but in making them in the first place. In making this distinction, Greenawalt largely appeals to the ideal of judicial objectivity—that a judge rendering a decision should set aside her personal views and follow a law's text, the legislature's intent, or the guidance of precedent. Many religious believers would agree with the ideal of judicial objectivity. But it is important to note here that the objective ideal excludes all views outside of those embodied in the governing law, and not just religious views.

On the other hand, the theory of legal realism has taught us that interpreting and applying the law is not a mechanical or wholly objective process, and that the personal views and experiences of judges are likely to affect their decisions. If such influences are deemed permissible (perhaps because they are unavoidable), can a judge then be equally influenced by religious values in making a decision? These are questions that have only begun to be explored, and that are likely to remain with us for a long time—as long as both law and religion speak to moral issues that are vitally important and yet deeply contested.

Conclusion

Religion has historically played an important role in American politics. For that reason, and perhaps to ensure that religious views are given equal treatment to secular ones, the Court has not struck down many laws on the ground that they lack a sufficiently "secular purpose." It has done so in some cases involving the public schools, but those may be unusual because the Court views the context as particularly sensitive and because most of the practices forbidden involved explicit religious elements: prayers and Bible readings, displays of the Ten Commandments, and the teaching of religious doctrines.

Some commentators have argued, however, that even if it is constitutional for laws to be based heavily on religious values, legislators generally should not do so as a matter of political morality or prudence. A variety of positions on this question have emerged in debate, from those who say there should be little or no reliance on distinctively religious reasons for legislating, to those who say such reliance is perfectly fine, to those who say that "ecumenical," "widely shared," or "reasoned" religious beliefs are appropriate in politics but narrower or more "sectarian" beliefs are not.

CHAPTER SEVEN
THE DEFINITION OF "RELIGION"

We now turn to address one additional question that cuts across all of the issues discussed in this book: what is the meaning of the term "religion" that is the subject of the First Amendment? The question arises under both Religion Clauses. What sort of activity by an individual or group is the exercise of "religion" and therefore protected by the Free Exercise Clause? And correspondingly, what sorts of ideas or practices are "religion" such that as the government cannot make a law respecting the establishment of them?

A. TRADITIONAL DEFINITIONS OF RELIGION

The complications raised by the need to define "religion" are more obvious now than they once were. For much of Western history in general, and American history in particular, "religion" was understood by most people solely as a set of beliefs and practices relating to a divine being, such as the God of Judaism and Christianity. At the time of the founding, for the vast majority of Americans, traditional theistic religions were the only belief systems that gave a comprehensive account of the nature of the universe and the meaning of human existence. Even Deism, the major competitor to traditional Christianity and Judaism during the founding period, affirmed belief in a divine being (albeit one who was relatively impersonal and did not intervene in the natural world or human affairs). And even many of the world religions that were known to Westerners but were still unfamiliar and exotic, such Hinduism, included beliefs about divine beings. Thus in one of the 19th-century cases involving the Mormon practice of polygamy, the Supreme Court defined religion as "one's views of his relations to his Creator, and to the obligations they impose of reverence for his being and character, and of obedience to his will." *Davis v. Beason* (S.Ct. 1890).

Although such statements implied that all beliefs in or about God would be deemed "religion," the Court sometimes appeared to have difficulty extending the concept even to theistic views if it regarded them as dangerous or primitive. *Davis* itself, for example, said that "[t]o call th[e] advocacy [of polygamy or bigamy] a tenet of religion is to offend the common sense of mankind"—even though the Mormons clearly understood polygamy as a practice ordained by God.

B. EXPANDED DEFINITIONS OF RELIGION

The theistic definition of religion has come under challenge in recent decades, however, because two other kinds of beliefs have become more common and more prominent in American culture than they once were. The first challenge comes from recognized world religions that do not believe in a divine being. The Supreme Court recognized, in a footnote in a 1961 decision, that a number of religions "do not teach what would generally be considered a belief in the existence of God," including "Buddhism, Taoism, Ethical Culture, [and] Secular Humanism." *Torcaso v. Watkins* (S.Ct.1961). These faiths have become more prevalent and noticeable in the United States in recent years, even though they remain small numerical minorities. *Torcaso,* in striking down a state requirement that public officials swear a belief in God, set forth the principle that the government may not favor "those religions based on a belief in the existence of God as against those religions founded on different beliefs."

The second challenge arises from philosophical views that are not theistic and are not even colloquially referred to as "religious," but that have some of the same features of traditional religion and that perform some of the same functions, for the persons that follow them, that traditional religions perform for their adherents. Some ideologies commonly thought of as secular provide an overarching explanation of human nature and history, a code of conduct for all believers to follow, and a set of symbols and to express the believer's identity. Marxism, for example, has claimed to explain and predict history by means of the theory of "dialectical materialism," and it often has required all adherents to devote themselves fully to the Marxist cause. In the last two centuries, such ideologies have become widespread in Western culture. At certain times among important parts of the population, such systems may even have become more influential than traditional religion: consider, for example, the influence that Freudianism and other psychological theories about human nature and the meaning of life have had in the twentieth century. And of course, individuals often mix religious ideas with other belief systems, in a bewildering variety of ways.

Should the definition of "religion" for legal purposes expand to take account of non-theistic religions, or even belief systems that have not been traditionally labeled as "religions"? This issue first came to the Supreme Court in the context not of the Religion Clauses, but of the federal statute exempting religious conscientious objectors from military service. The Draft Act of 1917 exempted persons affiliated with a "well-recognized religious sect or organization" whose tenets forbade participation in war. In the 1940s, Congress expanded the exemption to any individual, even outside a recognized sect, whose opposition to war stemmed from "religious training and belief"; but a legislative report accompanying the change defined that term still to include only "beliefs in a relation to a Supreme Being" and not "essentially political, sociological, or philosophical views or a merely personal moral code." However, during the Vietnam War the Court twice read this statute very broadly to extend exemptions to persons whose beliefs were not traditionally religious.

United States v. Seeger (S.Ct.1965), extended the exemption to a man who was an agnostic and whose opposition to war rested on "a belief in and devotion to goodness and virtue for their own sakes, and a religious faith in a purely ethical creed." The Court adopted a broad, "functional" definition of religion rather than a traditional one: a "sincere and meaningful belief which occupies in the life of its possessor a place parallel to that filled by the God of those admittedly qualifying for the exemption." The opinion noted the diversity of religions in America and cited a number of theologians and beliefs that regard God not as a distinct being but as "the highest ideal that [humans] can conceive," our "ultimate concern,"or "the ground of our very being." Under this test, the beliefs of Seeger and the other claimants were covered because they performed the same function as God in the lives of traditional believers. But the Court continued to maintain that a "merely personal moral code" would not count as religion, although it never really gave an example of the line that it was drawing.

Welsh v. United States (S.Ct.1970), went a step further and held that a claimant with beliefs similar to those of Seeger fit within the "religious training and belief" exemption even though he specifically insisted that his beliefs were not religious. The Court had deferred to the individual's understanding of his own beliefs in calling Seeger's beliefs religious; but it declined to defer to Welsh's self-understanding because he might not have been aware of the "broad scope" of the term as it had been interpreted.

Two concurring justices in these cases advanced an important argument as to why the statutory term "religious" should be read so broadly: if it were not, they said, it would violate the Establishment Clause and other constitutional provisions by favoring theistic religion over other conscientious bases for objecting to war. Justice Douglas in *Seeger* argued that theism could not be favored over other religions, such as Buddhism, that have no concept of a personal God. But Justice Harlan in *Welsh* pressed the argument further, saying that simply including non-theistic religions was not enough because the exemption would still favor religion over other bases for conscientious objection. (Douglas was willing to read the statute broadly to avoid the constitutional question. Harlan said the statute could not legitimately be read so broadly and was therefore unconstitutionally discriminatory; but he was willing to adopt the broad rule as a judicial remedy that would cure the discrimination without eliminating the "longstanding" and "important" policy of exempting conscientious objectors.)

The definitional issue raised in *Seeger* and *Welsh* thus returns us to the question, discussed at length in Chapter 3, of whether it is an unfair favoritism for the government to treat religiously-motivated actions different from actions motivated by other conscientiously held beliefs.

Some commentators have advanced another argument why the narrower exemption would be unconstitutional: it would require courts to delve deeply into the nature of a claimant's beliefs in order to decide whether they involved a Supreme Being or some analogous divine reality. Courts would thus have to make sensitive theological judgments in territory very unfamiliar to them, often second-guessing the believer's own understanding. The Supreme Court has emphasized that courts are not to be "arbiters of scriptural interpretation." *Thomas v. Review Board* (S.Ct.1981). Of course, one might respond that the Court's standard, focusing on the role or function that a belief plays for the adherent, requires just as much theological examination in order to determine whether that role is parallel to the role played by God in traditional religions.

The Vietnam decisions were readings of a single statute protecting religiously motivated behavior, and as such have authoritative force only for the interpretation of that statute. However, similar questions arise, and have more far-reaching import, under the general protection given by the Free Exercise Clause. Should "religion" in the Constitution be understood only to refer to beliefs with a content analogous to that of theism, or should it encompass any belief that plays a similar role or function in the believer's life? The Supreme Court touched on the issue in *Wisconsin v. Yoder* (S.Ct. 1972), holding that Amish parents and children had a free exercise right to be exempt from compulsory school laws, but stating that parents who withdrew their children from school on the basis of Thoreau's ideas would not be exempt because such a choice would be "philosophical and personal rather than religious." This statement suggested a retreat from the broad, "functional" view of religion set out in the Vietnam cases. But it was dicta (since the Amish views were conceded to be religious), and the Court has never revisited the issue.

Several courts of appeals have attempted expanded First Amendment definitions of religion. For example, in *Africa v. Pennsylvania* (3d Cir. 1981), the court set out three indicia that a belief system is religious: (1) it addresses "fundamental and ultimate questions" dealing with "deep and imponderable matters"; (2) it is "comprehensive" in its concerns rather than an "isolated teaching" on a particular issue; and (3) it may (though it need not have) "formal," "external signs" such as clergy, worship services, holy texts, and so forth.

The issue of defining religion has also arisen because of claims that the curriculum in public schools teaches the religion of "secular humanism" (which, as noted, above, the Supreme Court mentioned as a religion in *Torcaso v. Watkins*). Some theologically conservative Christians argue that the overarching ideology taught in schools is that there is no higher power or ultimate authority and that decisions about ethical behavior must be made according to the individual's own subjective views. The court of appeals decision that considered this contention, *Smith v. Board of Commissioners of Mobile County Schools* (11th Cir.1987), avoided the question whether secular humanism could be a religion, because it held that such an ideology was not being officially taught in the schools. The curriculum merely exposed students to various ideas and taught them skills of critical reasoning. Although such an approach might be consistent with some non-theistic ideologies and inconsistent with some religious beliefs, it did not itself constitute a comprehensive ideology analogous to a religion. Indeed, the challenged textbooks noted that many people derive their moral guidance from their religious beliefs.

Despite the arguments for broadening the constitutional definition to include all belief systems that are functionally very important to their adherents, such an expansion could also pose two problems. If applied under the Free Exercise Clause, it could lead to virtually limitless exemptions from laws because of the multiplicity of moral belief systems in America. And if applied under the Establishment Clause, a broad test could prevent government from promoting or teaching a great many views about moral or social questions. For example, if American patriotism could in some sense be seen as a religion, are public schools forbidden to try to inculcate love of country in their students?

The definitional problems may be less serious now that the Court has begun more and more to treat religion and other beliefs and practices equally under both the Free Exercise and Establishment Clauses. For example, if religiously motivated conduct is entitled to no more constitutional protection from laws than any other bases for the same conduct (see *Employment Division v. Smith*, Chapter 3), there is no need to define the meaning and scope of "religious" conduct. The same is true if religious speech is permitted in public schools or other institutions on the same terms as other speech (Chapter 4), or if religiously affiliated institutions can receive government assistance on the same terms as other institutions (Chapter 5). Indeed, one of the reasons that the Court has moved toward treating all belief systems equally may be that it believes that the difficulties in defining religion and distinguishing it from other views or activities are too great.

However, since public schools (and perhaps other government agencies) are still prohibited from conducting any official religious exercises or teaching any religion as true or false (Chapter 4), a broad definition of religion could still paralyze government in its efforts to teach or support moral goals.

C. RESOLVING THE DEFINITION PROBLEM

Commentators have tried to resolve the problem of defining religion in a way that is broad enough to recognize the increased variety of American faiths and yet is not so broad that it hampers government's ability to support various moral goals and policies or to or differentiate between them.

1. One possible solution, offered by Professor Laurence Tribe, is to define religion differently under the two clauses, free exercise and non-estab-

lishment. A belief would fall within free exercise protection, under Tribe's proposal, if it were only "arguably religious," but teaching the belief would be free from establishment limits if it were "arguably non-religious." However, Tribe's suggestion has been criticized on the ground that it is incompatible with the First Amendment's text: the word "religion" actually appears only once in the Amendment, encompassing both clauses (no law "respecting an establishment of religion, nor prohibiting the free exercise thereof").

Some of the practical advantages of Tribe's proposal might be achieved by a slightly different route, without taking the textually questionable step of defining religion differently under the two clauses. One might say that whether a belief involves the free exercise of religion is heavily affected by how the individual believer views its role in his life, but that whether a belief is a religious one being established by the government depends much more on how society understands it. Society may not understand a belief as being analogous to religion, even if some individuals understand it that way. However, even under this approach one still has to define what religion is.

2.   A second option would be to move back toward a more traditional understanding of religion as involving duties to a Supreme Being or at least duties imposed by some divine moral order. Those who argue for this position assert that it is more consistent with the framers' original understanding of the meaning of religion; in part they point to the

rejection of an earlier First Amendment draft that would have protected "liberty of conscience" (see Chapter 2). Proponents of this view also argue that the Constitution gives distinctive protection to religion because it is not simply another choice of moral views among the many that individuals can make, but because it involves a duty to a higher power that the believer is unable to avoid. Older formulations captured this idea. See, e.g., *United States v. Macintosh* (S.Ct.1931) (Hughes, C.J., dissenting) (religion is "a belief in a relation to God involving duties superior to those arising from any human relation"); see also Chapter 3 (discussing reasons for recognizing distinctive protection for religious practice against general laws). Without this unique feature of duty to a superior power, it is argued, there is no basis to treat religion differently from any other deeply-held moral belief (and the result is the demise of free exercise exemptions in *Employment Division v. Smith*).

This position might still recognize familiar non-theistic religions such as Buddhism. Moreover, it would still allow for the holding of non-theistic beliefs and the expression of them to be protected under the Free Speech Clause; government plainly could not punish Seeger and Welsh from publicly stating their conscientious opposition to the war. But if their serious non-theistic beliefs were not treated as religion, then they would not be entitled to an accommodation of their conduct in refusing to go to war.

Even under this narrower view, it could be argued that the definition of religion should extend to atheism (the view that God does not exist) or agnosticism (the view that nothing can be known about whether God exists). Although these views are in one sense opposed to "religion," they are like religion in that they specifically address, and are built around, the fundamental religious question of whether there is God or some divine reality. If these views were not treated as religion, then logically the government would be able to teach atheism explicitly in the schools, and to support it explicitly through official messages or through preferential funding. The communist government of the Soviet Union taught official atheism, but for an American public school or other government agency to teach explicitly that there is no God would seem blatantly inconsistent with the Religion Clauses.

Logically, then, if Seeger's and Welsh's objection to military service was related in some way to their belief in the non-existence of God, they might be able to raise a claim under the Free Exercise Clause even under this narrower view. But it was not clear that their moral opposition stemmed from any proposition specifically about God, as opposed to simply from their beliefs about the overall nature of humanity and morality.

We have already noted the primary criticism of the "narrower" definition of religion, which is that it assertedly favors theistic (and perhaps atheistic and agnostic) beliefs over other deeply held beliefs that cannot raise a claim for exemption from general laws.

3.   A third option is to continue to pursue some sort of expanded definition of religion that includes non-theistic views but does not go so far as to give constitutional status to every moral belief. An example is the court of appeals' definition in *Africa*, involving ultimacy, comprehensiveness, and external symbols. The court argued, for example, that its factors of ultimacy and comprehensiveness could distinguish religions, even non-theistic ones, from mere personal or philosophical views. The latter, the court said, will often be not comprehensive but instead focused on a particular issue or set of issues: for example, Marxism primarily focuses on economic and political matters and thus would not meet the test despite the fervor with which it is held by many of its adherents. The court seemed to be trying to expand the definition of religion, but still to preserve a limit that the content of the belief be analogous to traditional religion, and to require something more than that the belief be deeply important or meaningful to the adherent.

The *Africa* court applied these factors to a prisoner's claim that he should receive a special diet of uncooked food to accommodate his naturist philosophy and style of living. The court held that these views were not religious because they dealt almost entirely with personal health matters and social issues and thus were neither ultimate nor all-encompassing. The court said it could not distinguish Africa's beliefs from other "single-faceted ideologies

... such as economic determinism, Social Darwinism, or even vegetarianism," none of which would qualify as a First Amendment religion. Finally, the court noted that the group to which the prisoner belonged, called the MOVE, had none of the indicia of traditional religions such as holidays, services or ceremonies, scripture, or clergy. (The court conceded that this last factor could not be applied too strictly or else it would limit too greatly the variety of forms that religion could take.)

INDEX

References are to Pages

277

JUSTICES OF SUPREME COURT (INDIVIDUAL REFERENCES)
—Cont'd

Thomas, Clarence, 202
White, Byron, 144, 226

NEUTRALITY TOWARD RELIGION

Aid to religious entities and, 222–25
Criticisms of "neutrality," 30–31
"Formal" (equal treatment with non-religion), 21
Lemon test and, 29
School-sponsored religious exercises and, 152
"Substantive" (respecting religious choice), 21

OTHER FEDERAL CONSTITUTIONAL PROVISIONS AND DOC-TRINES

Amendment provision (Article V), 11
Equal Protection Clause, 249
Fourteenth Amendment section 5 (and RFRA), 125–26
"Substantive due process" rights, 64, 250–51
Supremacy Clause (Article VI, section 2), 10, 236

PERSONS (WRITERS, THEORISTS, STATESMEN)

Augustine, 37
Beecher, Lyman, 58
Bush, George, 1
Calvin, John, 38, 241
Constantine, 36
Elizabeth I, 40
Falwell, Jerry, 216
Greenawalt, Kent, 252, 258–59
Humphrey, Hubert, 243
Hutchinson, Anne, 41
Jefferson, Thomas, 15, 46–48, 52, 54, 75, 76, 200–01
Kant, Immanuel, 253
King, Martin Luther, 243
Laycock, Douglas, 21, 34
Lincoln, Abraham, 59, 156
Locke, John, 76
Luther, Martin, 38–39
Madison, James, 18, 21, 42, 46–50, 52, 54, 93, 200–02
McConnell, Michael, 88
Perry, Michael, 257–58
Smolin, David, 258
Thoreau, Henry David, 83, 85, 269
Tribe, Laurence, 271–72
Williams, Roger, 16, 29, 42–43, 68

RELIGIOUS TESTS FOR PUBLIC OFFICE—Cont'd
Free Exercise Clause and, 45, 71
Religious Test Clause (Article VI, section 3), 4, 45

SEPARATION OF CHURCH AND STATE
Aid to religious entities and, 23, 196, 206–07, 234
As fundamental Religion Clause value, 15–17
Clash with equal-treatment value, 24
Government-sponsored religious exercises and, 153
Institutional separation (limited), 15, 37–38
Lemon test and, 29
Original understanding an, 53
Political involvement of religion and, 240, 251
"Release time" programs and, 173
Religious speech by citizens in public institutions and, 73–75, 162–63
To protect religion's purity, 16–17, 53, 240, 243
To protect secular peace, 16
"Wall of separation" phrase (Thomas Jefferson), 15–16, 23

STATE CONSTITUTIONAL PROVISIONS ON RELIGION
Aid to religious entities and, 203–04, 234–36
Free exercise and, 129–31
Strict church-state separation and, 162

VALUES UNDERLYING RELIGION CLAUSES
Clashes between values, 22–25
Values described, 15–21